# HARVARD GRAPHICS FOR WINDOWS FOR DUMMIES™

Quick Referen[ce]



by Raymond E. Werner

IDG BOOKS

IDG Books Worldwide, Inc.
An International Data Group Company
Foster City, CA ♦ Chicago, IL ♦ Indianapolis, IN ♦ Braintree, MA ♦ Dallas, TX

**Harvard Graphics For Windows For Dummies Quick Reference**

Published by
**IDG Books Worldwide, Inc.**
An International Data Group Company
919 East Hillsdale Blvd.
Suite 400
Foster City, CA 94404



Library of Congress Catalog Card No.: 94-79836

ISBN: 1-56884-962-1

Printed in the United States of America

10 9 8 7 6 5 4 3 2 1 RS/QR/ZU

Distributed in the United States by IDG Books Worldwide, Inc.

Distributed in Canada by Macmillan of Canada, a Division of Canada Publishing Corporation; by Computer and Technical Books in Miami, Florida, for South America and the Caribbean; by Longman Singapore in Singapore, Malaysia, Thailand, and Korea; by Toppan Co. Ltd. in Japan; by Asia Computerworld in Hong Kong; by Woodslane Pty. Ltd. in Australia and New Zealand; and by Transworld Publishers Ltd. in the U.K. and Europe.

For general information on IDG Books in the U.S., including information on discounts and premiums, contact IDG Books at 800-434-3422 or 415-312-0650.

For information on where to purchase IDG Books outside the U.S., contact Christina Turner at 415-312-0650.

For information on translations, contact Marc Jeffrey Mikulich, Director of Foreign & Subsidiary Rights, at IDG Books Worldwide, 415-312-0650.

For sales inquiries and special prices for bulk quantities, write to the address above or call IDG Books Worldwide at 415-312-0650.

For information on using IDG Books in the classroom, or for ordering examination copies, contact Jim Kelly at 800-434-2086.

# About the Author

Ray Werner is a freelance editor and author of *Word For Windows For Dummies, CorelDRAW! 5 For Dummies Quick Reference, The First Book of CorelDRAW! 3,* and *50 Ways to Get Your Money's Worth From Prodigy.* In his spare time, he is Adjunct Faculty at Ivy Tech State College in Indianapolis, teaching in the Applied Office Technology and Computer and Information Science departments. He can be reached on CompuServe at 71730,300.

# ABOUT IDG BOOKS WORLDWIDE

Welcome to the world of IDG Books Worldwide.

IDG Books Worldwide, Inc. is a subsidiary of International Data Group, the world's largest publisher of computer-related information and the leading global provider of information services on information technology. IDG was founded more than 25 years ago and now employs more than 7,000 people worldwide. IDG publishes more than 220 computer publications in 65 countries (see listing below). More than fifty million people read one or more IDG publications each month.

Launched in 1990, IDG Books Worldwide is today the #1 publisher of best-selling computer books in the United States. We are proud to have received 3 awards from the Computer Press Association in recognition of editorial excellence, and our best-selling *...For Dummies*™ series has more than 12 million copies in print with translations in 25 languages. IDG Books, through a recent joint venture with IDG's Hi-Tech Beijing, became the first U.S. publisher to publish a computer book in the People's Republic of China. In record time, IDG Books has become the first choice for millions of readers around the world who want to learn how to better manage their businesses.

Our mission is simple: Every IDG book is designed to bring extra value and skill-building instructions to the reader. Our books are written by experts who understand and care about our readers. The knowledge base of our editorial staff comes from years of experience in publishing, education, and journalism — experience which we use to produce books for the '90s. In short, we care about books, so we attract the best people. We devote special attention to details such as audience, interior design, use of icons, and illustrations. And because we use an efficient process of authoring, editing, and desktop publishing our books electronically, we can spend more time ensuring superior content and spend less time on the technicalities of making books.

You can count on our commitment to deliver high-quality books at competitive prices on topics consumers want to read about. At IDG, we value quality, and we have been delivering quality for more than 25 years. You'll find no better book on a subject than an IDG book.

John Kilcullen
President and CEO
IDG Books Worldwide, Inc.

VIII
WINNER
*Eighth Annual Computer Press Awards 1992*

IX
WINNER
*Ninth Annual Computer Press Awards 1993*

IDG Books Worldwide, Inc. is a subsidiary of International Data Group, the world's largest publisher of computer-related information and the leading global provider of information services on information technology. International Data Group publishes over 220 computer publications in 65 countries. More than fifty million people read one or more International Data Group publications each month. The officers are Patrick J. McGovern, Founder and Board Chairman; Kelly Conlin, President; Jim Casella, Chief Operating Officer. International Data Group's publications include: ARGENTINA'S Computerworld Argentina, Infoworld Argentina; AUSTRALIA'S Computerworld Australia, Computer Living, Australian PC World, Australian Macworld, Network World, Mobile Business Australia, Publish!, Reseller, IDG Sources; AUSTRIA'S Computerwelt Oesterreich, PC Test; BELGIUM'S Data News (CW); BOLIVIA'S Computerworld; BRAZIL'S Computerworld, Connections, Game Power, Mundo Unix, PC World, Publish, Super Game; BULGARIA'S Computerworld Bulgaria, PC & Mac World Bulgaria, Network World Bulgaria; CANADA'S CIO Canada, Computerworld Canada, InfoCanada, Network World Canada, Reseller; CHILE'S Computerworld Chile, Informatica; COLOMBIA'S Computerworld Colombia, PC World; COSTA RICA'S PC World; CZECH REPUBLIC'S Computerworld, Elektronika, PC World; DENMARK'S Communications World, Computerworld Danmark, Computerworld Focus, Macintosh Produktkatalog, Macworld Danmark, PC World Danmark, PC Produktguide, Tech World, Windows World; ECUADOR'S PC World Ecuador; EGYPT'S Computerworld (CW) Middle East, PC World Middle East; FINLAND'S MikroPC, Tietoviikko, Tietoverkko; FRANCE'S Distributique, GOLDEN MAC, InfoPC, Le Guide du Monde Informatique, Le Monde Informatique, Telecoms & Reseaux; GERMANY'S Computerwoche, Computerwoche Focus, Computerwoche Extra, Electronic Entertainment, Gamepro, Information Management, Macwelt, Netzwelt, PC Welt, Publish, Publish; GREECE'S Publish & Macworld; HONG KONG'S Computerworld Hong Kong, PC World Hong Kong; HUNGARY'S Computerworld SZT, PC World; INDIA'S Computers & Communications; INDONESIA'S Info Komputer; IRELAND'S ComputerScope; ISRAEL'S Beyond Windows, Computerworld Israel, Multimedia, PC World Israel; ITALY'S Computerworld Italia, Lotus Magazine, Macworld Italia, Networking Italia, PC Shopping Italy, PC World Italia; JAPAN'S Computerworld Today, Information Systems World, Macworld Japan, Nikkei Personal Computing, SunWorld Japan, Windows World; KENYA'S East African Computer News; KOREA'S Computerworld Korea, Macworld Korea, PC World Korea; LATIN AMERICA'S GamePro; MALAYSIA'S Computerworld Malaysia, PC World Malaysia; MEXICO'S Compu Edicion, Compu Manufactura, Computacion/Punto de Venta, Computerworld Mexico, MacWorld, Mundo Unix, PC World, Windows; THE NETHERLANDS' Computer! Totaal, Computable (CW), LAN Magazine, Lotus Magazine, MacWorld; NEW ZEALAND'S Computer Buyer, Computerworld New Zealand, Network World, New Zealand PC World; NIGERIA'S PC World Africa; NORWAY'S Computerworld Norge, Lotusworld Norge, Macworld Norge, Maxi Data, Networld, PC World Ekspress, PC World Nettverk, PC World Norge, PC World's Produktguide, Publish& Multimedia World, Student Data, Unix World, Windowsworld; PAKISTAN'S PC World Pakistan; PANAMA'S PC World Panama; PERU'S Computerworld Peru, PC World; PEOPLE'S REPUBLIC OF CHINA'S China Computerworld, China Infoworld, China PC Info Magazine, Computer Fan, PC World China, Electronics International, Electronics Today/Multimedia World, Electronic Product World, China Network World, Software World Magazine, Telecom Product World, PHILIPPINES' Computerworld Philippines, PC Digest (PCW); POLAND'S Computerworld Poland, Computerworld Special Report, Networld, PC World/Komputer, Sunworld; PORTUGAL'S Cerebro/PC World, Correio Informatico/Computerworld, MacIn; ROMANIA'S Computerworld, PC World, Telecom Romania; RUSSIA'S Computerworld-Moscow, Mir - PK (PCW), Sety (Networks); SINGAPORE'S Computerworld Southeast Asia, PC World Singapore; SLOVENIA'S Monitor Magazine; SOUTH AFRICA'S Computer Mail (CIO),Computing S.A.,Network World S.A., Software World; SPAIN'S Advanced Systems, Amiga World, Computerworld Espana, Communicaciones World, Macworld Espana, NeXTWORLD, Super Juegos Magazine (GamePro), PC World Espana, Publish; SWEDEN'S Attack, ComputerSweden, Corporate Computing, Macworld, Mikrodatorn, Natverk & Kommunikation, PC World, CAP & Design, Datalngenjoren, Maxi Data,Windows World; SWITZERLAND'S Computerworld Schweiz, Macworld Schweiz, PC Tip; TAIWAN'S Computerworld Taiwan, PC World Taiwan; THAILAND'S Thai Computerworld; TURKEY'S Computerworld Monitor, Macworld Turkiye, PC World Turkiye; UKRAINE'S Computerworld, Computers+Software Magazine; UNITED KINGDOM'S Computing /Computerworld, Connexion/Network World, Lotus Magazine, Macworld, Open Computing/Sunworld; URAGUAY'S PC World Uraguay; UNITED STATES' Advanced Systems, AmigaWorld, Cable in the Classroom, CD Review, CIO, Computerworld, Computerworld Client/Server Journal, Digital Video, DOS World, Electronic Entertainment Magazine (E2), Federal Computer Week, Game Hits, GamePro, IDG Books, Infoworld, Laser Event, Macworld, Maximize, Multimedia World, Network World, PC Letter, PC World, Publish, SWATPro, Video Event; VENEZUELA'S Computerworld Venezuela, PC World; VIETNAM'S PC World Vietnam. 11-16-94

IDG BOOKS

## Dedication

To Gloria King and all of the neat people at Ivy Tech State College. They let me play and are kind enough to call it teaching.

## Acknowledgments

There are always gobs of people to thank for any effort as intense as this one. Primarily, I would like to thank my editor, Greg Robertson. He proved to all of us that it is possible to juggle umpteen things at the same time and not drop any of them.

Tracy Barr did a great job of hand-holding, and — as always — I keep getting deeper and deeper into karma debt to Diane Steele and Mary Bednarek. Great people.

(The publisher would like to thank Patrick J. McGovern, without whom this book would not have been possible.)

# *Credits*

**Executive Vice President, Strategic Product Planning and Research**
David Solomon

**Editorial Director**
Diane Graves Steele

**Acquisitions Editor**
Megg Bonar

**Brand Manager**
Judith A. Taylor

**Editorial Managers**
Tracy L. Barr
Sandra Blackthorn

**Editorial Assistants**
Tamara S. Castleman
Stacey Holden Prince
Kevin Spencer

**Acquisitions Assistant**
Suki Gear

**Production Director**
Beth Jenkins

**Associate Project Coordinator**
Valery Bourke

**Pre-Press Coordinator**
Steve Peake

**Editors**
Greg Robertson
Pamela Mourouzis

**Technical Reviewer**
Larry Barr

**Production Staff**
Paul Belcastro
Mary Breidenbach
Chris Collins
Tyler Connor
Carla Radzakinas
Dwight Ramsey
Patricia R. Reynolds
Gina Scott

**Proofreader**
Betty Kish

**Indexer**
Anne Leach

**Cover Design**
Kavish + Kavish

## Contents at a Glance

## Table of Contents

# Introduction

I went to Ohio State and have never had a great amount of love for anything Ivy League. I also lived in Boston for a number of years, right next to Fenway Park and real close to MIT, Harvard, Boston College, and several gross more of those foliage-encrusted homes of higher learning, and even still higher chins — especially when talking to someone from the Midwest. (Many thought we still carried around all our worldly possessions in covered wagons.)

Although I almost hate to admit it, Harvard Graphics is terminally boss. So wonderful, in fact, that I have had a hard time writing this book because I keep stopping to play with the program, enjoying myself immensely, and being a pest to my computer buds and anyone else who will watch my presentations without threatening my life.

I think that you'll enjoy the program, too. It is a great way to use multimedia without spending absolutely oodles of bucks — although *almost* oodles makes it more fun. I mean, you gotta have a good sound card, a great video card, a CD-ROM drive, a dedicated TV, VCR, amplifier, color printer, 24-bit color scanner, and a VGA-to-TV translator, don't you? Not really, but don't tell on me, OK?

## About this book

This book is broken into two parts, each representing one of the programs that you got when you bought the SPG package: Harvard Graphics and Harvard F/X.

Each part is further broken in half into subparts, one on the commands and the other on the tools. I assume that you have some familiarity with the programs, because this is not a tutorial. The Quick Reference is really for folks who need to know what *that* does or how to use a particular command. If you are interested in a fun way to learn about the program, run down to your favorite bookstore and pick up a copy of *Harvard Graphics For Windows For Dummies* (Roger C. Parker, IDG Books Worldwide).

## What the funny little pictures mean

Each command has two little icons after it. The first gives you a clue as to the usefulness of the command, and the second is my purely arbitrary judgment about its safety. Here is what they mean:

This guy is cool. He tells you that the command is worth learning about and probably won't get you into a lot of trouble.

This guy is only somewhat cool. He lets you know that beginners may never really have to use the command or that slight potential for trouble exists.

Throw it to the lions. This command just isn't horribly useful, and you may be better served by trying to learn something else.

No worries. Shouldn't offer you the opportunity to get into any trouble.

If you're the worrisome type, you may want to be a little bit cautious. You can get into some trouble with these commands, but if you're careful, they shouldn't be fatal.

Tread softly. This icon notes the commands that made my system crash. They could wreak similar havoc on yours, too.

This icon points to operations and procedures that may cause disaster, or at least minor trauma. Watch out! Back up!

Useful, fascinating, and time-saving information follows this icon.

This icon refers you to another section of this book for more information.

This icon refers you to a relevant section of *Harvard Graphics For Windows For Dummies.* Hey, cross-marketing is where the bucks are (and you just might gain something from it).

OK, then … without further ado and saccharine cuteness, here goes.

# Part I

# Harvard Graphics

Harvard Graphics is a single-purpose program. It is dedicated to helping you create the most totally awesome and sophisticated presentations that you can imagine, while still allowing them to run on a computer that's not faster than greased lightning. You can get away quite easily with an 80386 running Windows 3.1 and having only 4MB of RAM and only 10MB or so of free disk space.

Such a system is protozoan by today's standards, but it is what quite a few people have. Of course, the program works better with more current equipment, but that's not the idea. You probably need presentations that you can take on the road, being sure that they can run on equipment that you will beg, borrow, or rent when you get where you need to be. If so, Harvard Graphics is for you.

TIP

Harvard Graphics offers three different ways to look at what you are doing: Slide Editor, Slide Sorter, and Outliner. Because you'll do the majority of work in the Slide Editor, the discussion of commands assumes that this is where you are unless the instructions tell you differently.

# Add Chart to Slide

## From Gallery

## Chart types listed

Adds a chart to the current slide. This command offers two options: From Gallery and the selection of a specific chart type. Choosing From Gallery opens the Gallery dialog box.

## Using Add chart to slide

To select a chart from the chart gallery:

1. Choose Add chart to slide from the Chart menu.
2. Choose From Gallery from the flyout menu to open the Chart Gallery dialog box.

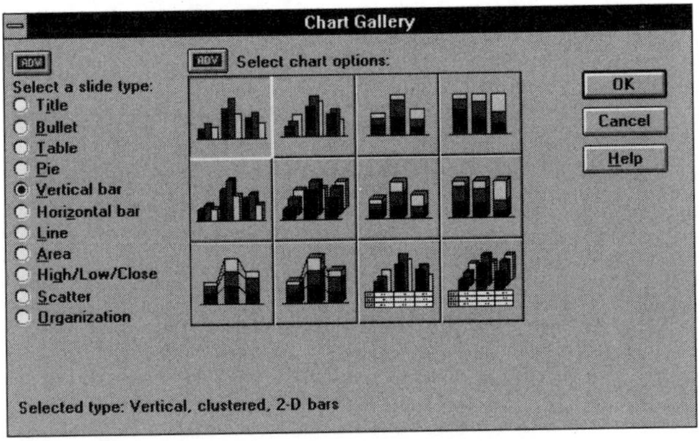


3. Select the chart type you want from the gallery.
4. Click OK to open the data entry form for the chart.

To select a specific chart type:

1. Choose Add chart to slide from the Chart menu.
2. Select the desired chart type from the Add chart to slide flyout menu to open the chart's data entry form.

## More stuff

You can use gobs of different options for charting. Use the Advisor to help you determine which type of chart is best for your data.

# Add Slide

Adds slides to your presentation.

## Toolbar icon

Add slide...

This one's not really on the toolbar, but click the Add slide button in the lower-right corner of the screen to add a new slide.

## Using Add slide

To add a slide to a presentation:

1. Choose Add slide from the Slide menu to open the Add Slide dialog box.

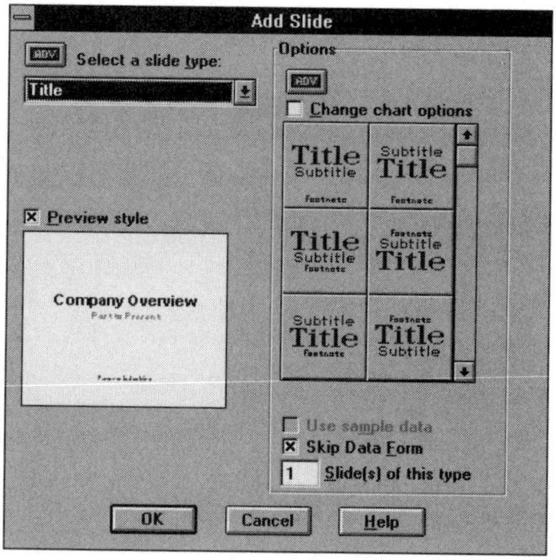


2. Select the type of slide that you want to add from the Select a slide type drop-down list.
3. Check the Preview style check box to see a representation of the slide type in the preview area.

4. If you prefer to use one of the variants of the selected chart type shown in the options area of the Add Slide dialog box, click it. This action automatically checks the Change chart options check box and uses the selected variation.
5. If your chart displays data, such as a line, bar, or pie chart, check the Use sample data check box to open a Data Form with sample numbers plugged in that you can change.
6. If you don't want to mess with a Data Form, check the Skip Data Form check box.
7. If you want to add more than one slide of the selected type, enter the number that you want in the Slide(s) of this type box.
8. Click OK to open the slide or Data Form.

## More stuff

TIP

Click the Advisor button above the Select a slide type drop-down list box to see which type of slide is best for the data you want to display.

Click the Advisor button in the Options area for a description of the available chart variations.

# Add Sound

Adding sound makes your presentations sing, talk, or grunt. It's a whole bunch of fun — if you're willing to spend the bucks for a sound card, mike, CD Reader, amplifier, tape deck, and other toys that this feature gives you the excuse to buy. You can easily make a sound bite cost about $1,000 a second, therefore qualifying you for the next open seat in Congress.

## Add Sound to Slide dialog box

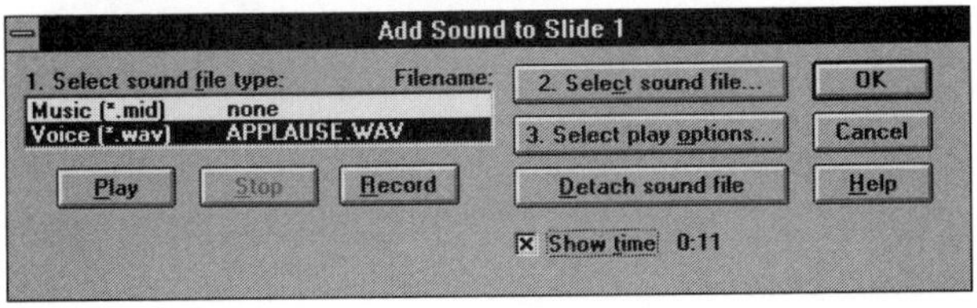

## Using Add sound

You can't add sound to a slide unless your system has been set up to record or play sounds in the Windows environment.

TIP: You need to consider one problem when you are adding sound to your presentations: If you want to play the presentation on another computer, that computer must be equipped with a sound card, too.

To add sound to a slide:

1. Choose Add sound from the Slide menu to open the Add Sound to Slide dialog box.
2. Select sound file type: either Music or Voice.
3. Select the sound file you want by clicking the Select sound file button to open a directory tree and finding and double-clicking the file's name.

   *or*

   Record your own sound by clicking the Record button. Then give the file a name, pull out the mike, and go to town.

   TIP: If you are really into sound, you probably will want to do your recording in the WAV or MID software that you are most familiar with. After you finish recording the sound, you can import the file into your presentation.
4. After you select the file, click the Select play options button to open the Play Options dialog box.

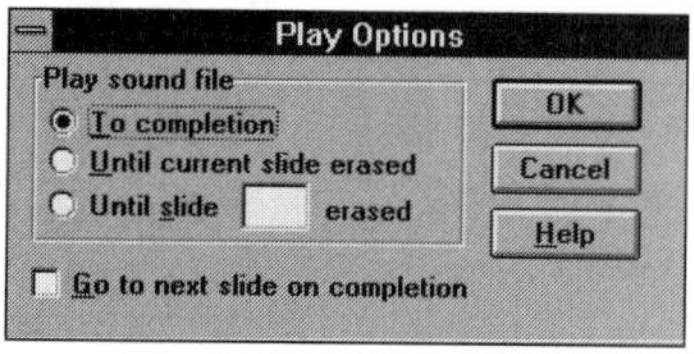


5. Choose the duration of the sound file in the Play Options dialog box.

To remove a sound file from a slide:

1. Choose Add sound from the Slide menu to open the Add Sound to Slide dialog box.
2. Select the sound you want to delete in the Select sound file type list.
3. Click the Detach sound file button.

### More stuff

TIP

Here's a neato way to avoid the trouble of transporting digital presentations and worrying about sound cards and the like: If your presentation does not require user input, you can use a VCR and one of the available VGA-to-TV translators to copy your presentation to video tape, sound effects and all.

## Add Stamp

I don't know why they call these things *stamps*. You would think that they would have called them *add date* or *add slide number*, but they didn't. Anyway, you use stamps to add date or slide number information to all slides in a presentation. You add stamps to the master template.

### Using Add stamp

To add a stamp to a presentation:

1. Choose Edit master template from the Style menu to open the master template.
2. Select the text tool.
3. Position the I-beam cursor where you want the stamp to be placed and then click the left mouse button.
4. Choose Add stamp from the Text menu and select the information you want the stamp to contain from the flyout menu.
5. When the stamp is complete, click outside the stamp area to close the text box.
6. Click Back to slide in the lower-right corner of the screen to leave the master template.

## Add Titles / Footnote

This command lets you "change your other mind" if you have deleted a title, subtitle, or footnote from a slide.

## Using Add titles / footnote

This command becomes available when one of the default titles has been deleted from a slide. Selecting it adds the deleted title or footnote back to the slide.

All you have to do is choose Add titles / footnote from the Slide menu.

# Add/Edit HyperShow Button

HyperShow buttons enable you to establish branches in your presentation, play sound files, or perform actions. You can create HyperShow buttons from existing objects, such as a picture, or you can simply add a normal-looking button. In either case, clicking the button or object initiates the event that is assigned to it.

## Ribbon bar icon

## Add/Edit HyperShow Button dialog box

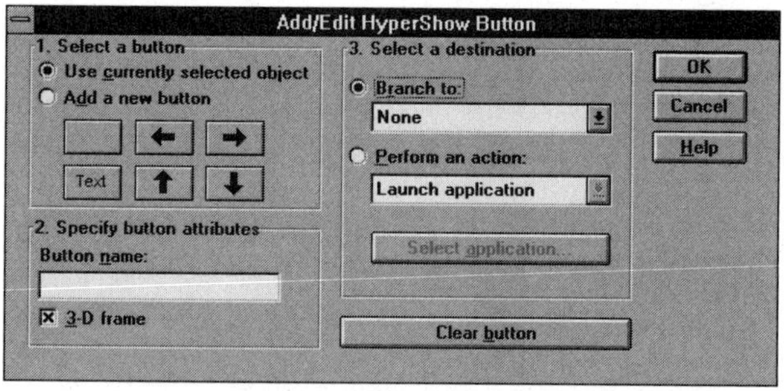


## Using Add/Edit HyperShow button

To add a HyperShow button created from an existing object:

1. In Slide Editor view, select the object you want to use.
2. Choose Add/Edit HyperShow button from the Slide menu to open the Add/Edit HyperShow Button dialog box.

3. Click the Use currently select object radio button if it is not already selected.
4. Give the button a name in the Button name box.

To use the button to send the presentation to another slide:

1. Click the Branch to radio button and select the slide to branch to from the drop-down list.
2. Click OK.

To use the button to perform an action:

1. Click the Perform an action radio button and select the action from the drop-down list. Doing so enables the Select application button.
2. Click the Select application button to open a directory tree and choose the application, sound file, or OLE action that you want to link to the button.
3. Click OK.

To add a standard button to the slide:

1. Choose Add/Edit HyperShow button from the Slide menu to open the Add/Edit HyperShow Button dialog box.
2. Click the Add a new button radio button.
3. Select the type of button you want and then follow the same procedure for adding a HyperShow button created from an existing object, starting with Step 4.

## More stuff

The button names don't appear on the slide. You can use the text tool to add a description of what the button does to the slide, or you can click the Text button to include a caption on the button's top.

See HyperShow Links to find out how to create HyperShow links by using keys and mouse buttons.

# Adopt Master Template

This command goes to show that even people who "paak the caa in the Haavaad yaad" are not immune to errors. The command would makes bunches more sense if it were called *Adapt* Master Template. Gad, how could anyone from Boston drop an *a*?

Use this command to override master template selections for a slide or group of slides.

## Using Adopt master template

1. Choose Adopt master template from the Slide menu to open the Master Template Options dialog box.

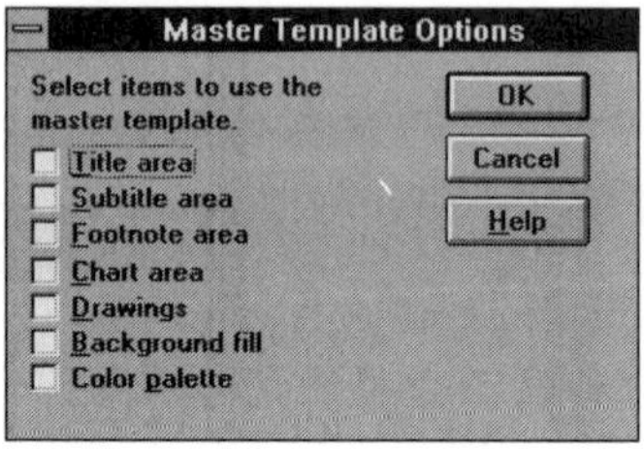


2. Check those boxes that represent things that you do *not* want to change from the master template.

   Cool. I suppose that you adopt parameters from the master template by checking the box — only an Ivy Leaguer or lawyer would turn stuff so far around that the argument is backward and still makes some kind of sense.

3. Click OK.

# Advisor

The Advisor is a wizened, old silicon chip that lives in a dark place hidden in the code of Harvard Graphics. Its purpose in life is to rule on the beauty and elegance of your work. It can be a royal pain. The Advisor command toggles display of the advisor on and off.

When toggled on, the Advisor information area appears on the right side of the screen. When off, the Advisor goes back into its hiding place and stops bothering you.

## Using Advisor

To make the Advisor information area visible or invisible, choose Advisor from the View menu.

## More stuff

Version 3.0 includes a Check Design feature. This feature reviews each slide in your show and gives you hints about any problems it sees.

# Align

Aligns the selection handles on two or more objects.

## Align dialog box

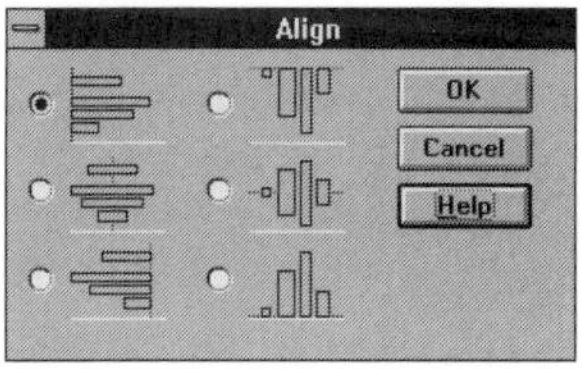

## Using Align

To line up two or more objects:

1. Select the objects by Shift+clicking each in turn.
2. Choose Align from the Graphics menu to open the Align dialog box.
3. Click the button next to the picture that represents how you want the objects to align.
4. Click OK.

## More stuff

TIP: Objects align on the selection handles. If, for example, you have a text object selected and its box is larger than the text it contains, the alignment takes place according to the box, not the text. This method can leave the text alignment looking pretty ugly. To fix this problem, resize the text box to conform to the length of the text in it before selecting it.

TIP: To align objects both horizontally and vertically, center them on the horizontal handles and then choose Align Again and select the vertical ones. (You are doing Step 3 twice.)

REFERENCE: To center objects in the slide, see Center on Slide.

# All Attributes

Even though you can set text attributes individually by using the Font, Size, Style, and Color commands, using them can become quite a pain if you want to change more than one attribute at a time. The All attributes command opens a handy dialog box that lets you change multiple attributes at the same time.

## Attribute bar icon

## Text Attributes dialog box

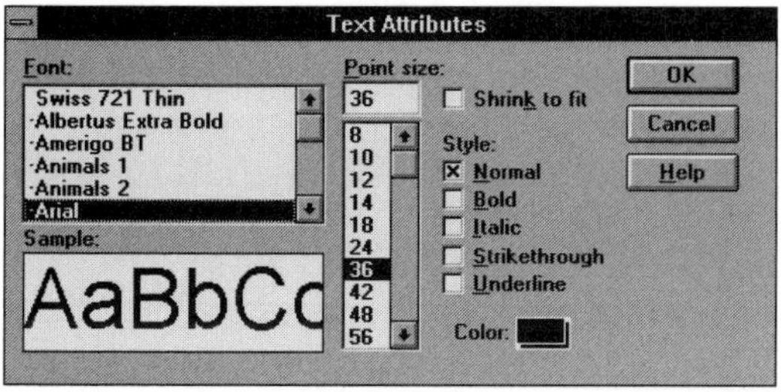


## Using All attributes

To change the attributes of existing text:

1. Select the text box(es) with the selection tool.
2. Choose All attributes from the Text menu.
3. Choose the Font, Point size, Color, and Style you want.
4. Click the Shrink to fit box if you want the font size to automatically reduce to fit the text box.

## More stuff

TIP

If you make any changes in the Text Attributes dialog box without first selecting any text, you also change the defaults for subsequent text boxes.

# Attribute Bar

The attribute bar is a great place to go when you need to change text attributes, line attributes, or fill attributes. Nice as it is, there are times when you may prefer for it not to hang around taking up valuable screen space. The Attribute bar command takes it out of the neighborhood (makes it invisible) until you want it to come back.

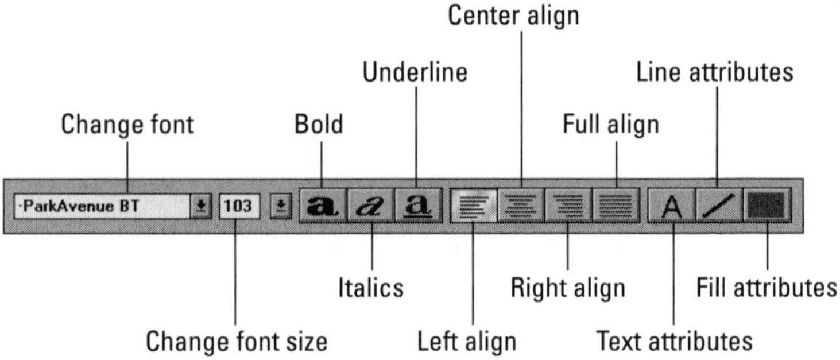


## Using Attribute bar

To display or hide the attribute bar, choose Attribute bar from the View menu.

# Autobuild

You use Autobuild to construct a series of slides that builds upon itself. A speaker uses Autobuild when he or she clicks that little clicker doodad and bullet points appear one by one, a pie is assembled piece by piece, or a chart is built item by item on-screen. Autobuilding is really neat and easy to do.

## Autobuild dialog box

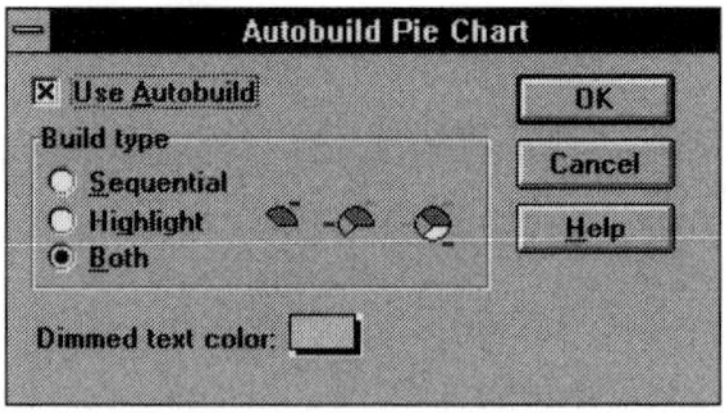


## Using Autobuild

1. Construct the complete chart or bullet list.
2. Make sure that the slide is displayed in the Slide Editor or is selected in the Slide Sorter.

3. Choose Autobuild from the Slide menu to open the Autobuild dialog box.

   TIP

   The Autobuild dialog box title varies with the kind of slide selected. The options are all the same, however.

4. Click the Use Autobuild check box to select it.
5. Choose the Build type you want.
   - **Sequential:** A Sequential build brings one element — a pie slice, for example — into the chart at a time.
   - **Highlight:** A Highlight build dims all elements of the chart other than the one being introduced. The entire chart appears, but different segments stand out one at a time.
   - **Both:** Choosing Both brings one element in at a time, leaving all previous elements displayed but dimmed.
6. Click the Dimmed text color box to open a color selection palette if you want to change the color of text when it is not highlighted.
7. Choose OK.

## More stuff

TIP

Autobuild does not work on title slides, high/low/close charts, organization charts, or drawings. It also does not function on slides that contain more than one chart.

The easiest way to view your creation is to click the ScreenShow from current slide icon in the toolbar. Press Enter to cycle through the Autobuild; press Esc to exit the Slide view.

# Autosave

Don't get me wrong: Autosave is a great idea, but I find it a royal pain in the patootie. If you frequently forget to save your work, or if you are the kind of computist who gets mad and throws things if you lose several hours of work, Autosave may be the answer for you. On the other hand, if you are the kind of person who needs to be in control (like me) and doesn't like electromechanical servants being uppity (like me), turn this command off.

## Autosave dialog box

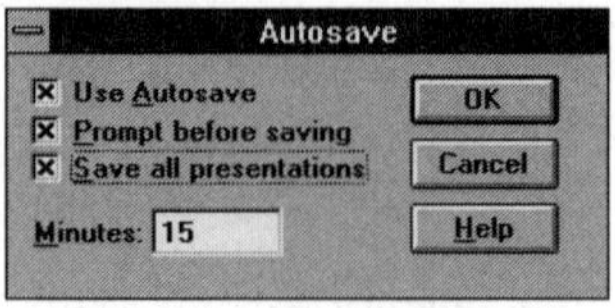


## Using Autosave

1. To open the Autosave dialog box, choose Autosave from the Options menu.
2. Decide to what extent you want to be pestered.
   - Deselect, or take the X out of, the Use Autosave check box if you don't want to be pestered at all.
   - Select, or put an X in, the Use Autosave check box if you enjoy being interrupted in the middle of something important.
3. Choose how much power over your life you want to give the computer.
   - Select the Prompt before saving check box if you enjoy having your computer ask permission to do what you told it to do in the first place.
   - Deselect the Prompt before saving check box if you want the machine just to go ahead and get it over with.
   - Select the Save all presentations check box if you want to Autosave all open presentations and you don't mind waiting around while the machine happily complies.
   - Deselect the Save all presentations check box if you want to Autosave only the current presentation.
4. Establish how often you want to be pestered by your silicone-based life form by putting some arbitrary time interval in the Minutes box.
5. Click OK.

## More stuff

TIP

After an Autosave, you can't undo the last actions you performed before Autosaving.

Autosave functions only when Harvard Graphics is the active application.

# Axis

Use this command to name, scale, and configure chart axes.

## Axis dialog box

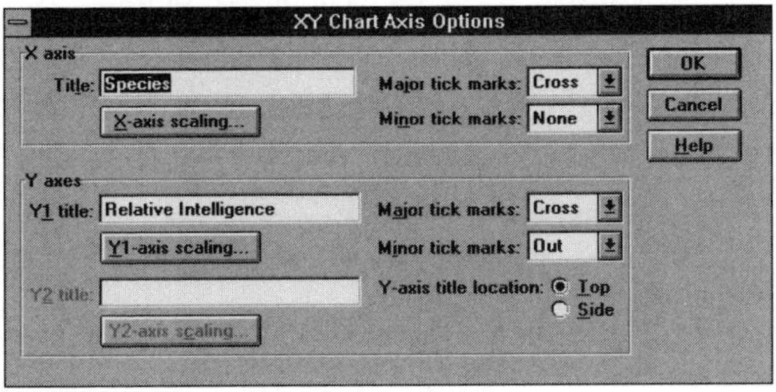


## Using Axis

1. Select the chart that you want to modify (this command works only on charts that have axes).
2. Choose Axis from the Chart menu to open the Axis Options dialog box.
3. Place the name of the X-axis in the X-axis title box and the Y-axis name(s) in the Y1 or Y2 title box.
4. If the axes contain numerical information, you can establish a scale for them by clicking the appropriate axis scaling button to open the Scaling Options dialog box.

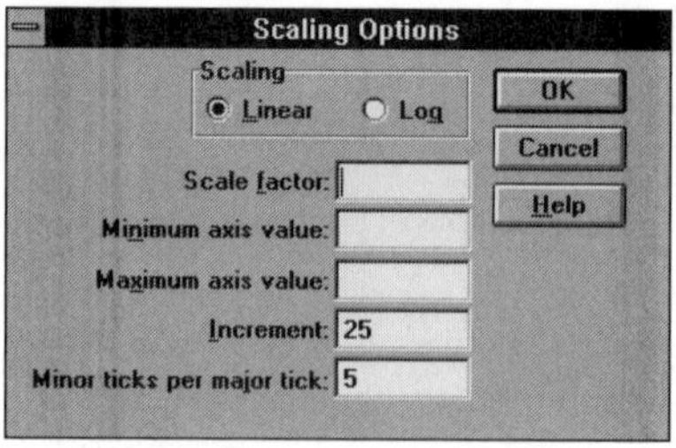


- Use a Linear scale if your number series is relatively compact.
- Use a Log (logarithmic) scale if your number series is spread out.
- Scale factor divides your number series by the number entered here to "tighten up" the display.
- Minimum and Maximum axis values set the starting and ending points on the axis scale.
- Increment establishes the major divisions on the chart.
- Minor ticks per major tick establishes the number of hash marks between the major divisions on the axis scale.
- The Major tick marks and Minor tick marks drop-down lists determine how the line that shows the tick mark intersects with the axis line. The choices are Come in from the axis line, Go out from the axis line, or Cross the axis line.

5. Choose OK to finish off the chart.

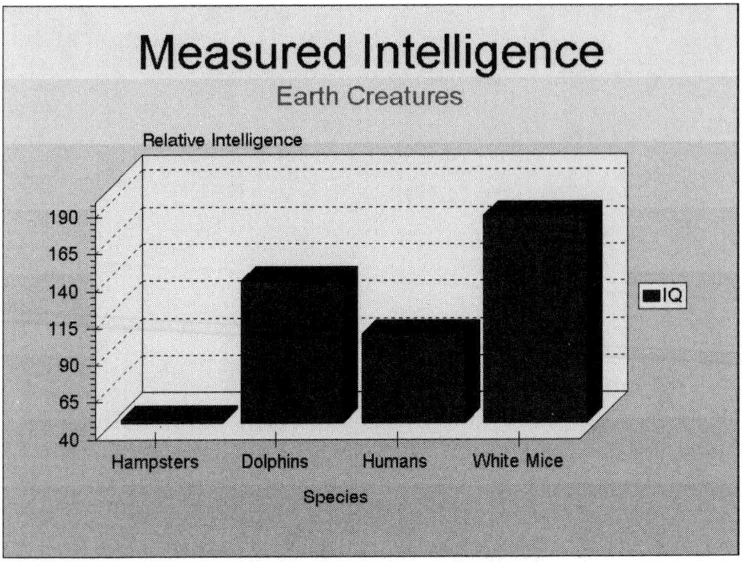


## B&W Preview

Allows you to view your slide in glorious black and white.

### Digital rodent replacement

Shift + F2

### Using B&W preview

Choose B&W preview from the View menu.

### More stuff

It's fast.

# Background

## Solid

## Hatch / Pattern

## Gradient

## Bitmap

## Images

Use this command to change or create the background for your slides.

## Using Background

Choose Background from the Style menu to open the flyout menu.

For uniform color fills:

1. Choose Solid to select a uniform color for the fill from the Solid Color Fill dialog box.

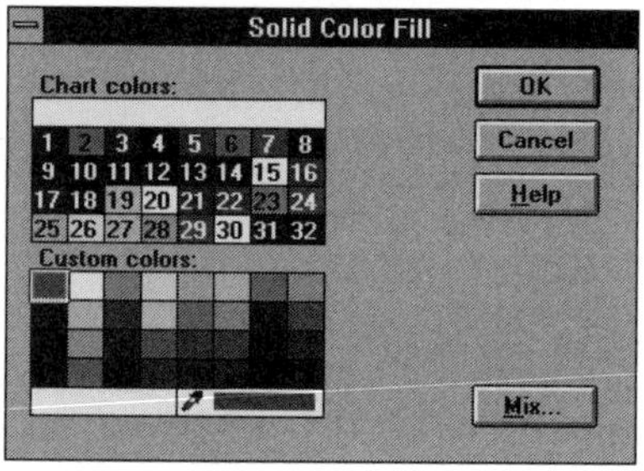


2. Click the color you want in the palette, or click the Mix button to create a custom color in the Mix Custom Colors dialog box.

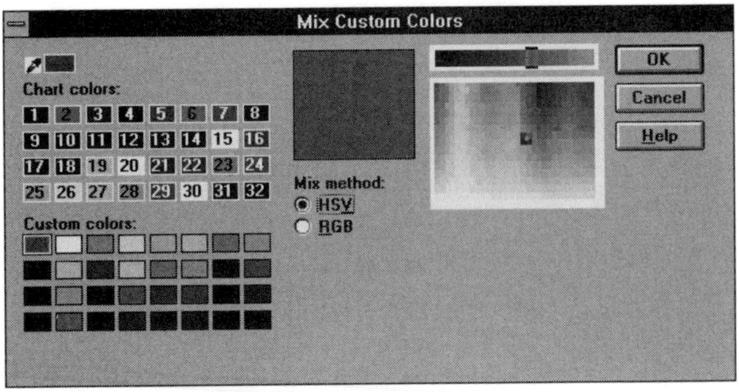


3. Drag the sliders until the color you want appears in the preview area, and then click OK twice to apply the color to the slide.

For hatch or pattern fills:

1. Choose Hatch / Pattern from the Background flyout menu to open the Hatch / Pattern Fill dialog box.

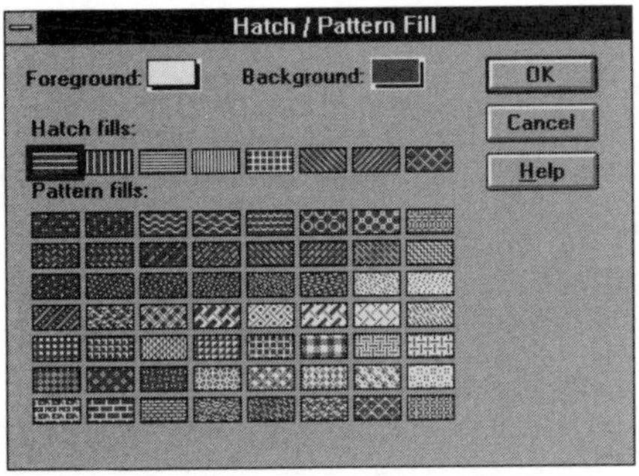


2. Click the Foreground and Background color boxes to select the colors that you want. You can mix custom colors the same way as in the Solid Color Fill dialog box described in the preceding series of steps.
3. Click the hatch or pattern fill that you want.
4. Click OK to apply your selections.

For Gradient fills:

1. Choose Gradient from the Background flyout menu to open the Gradient Fill dialog box.

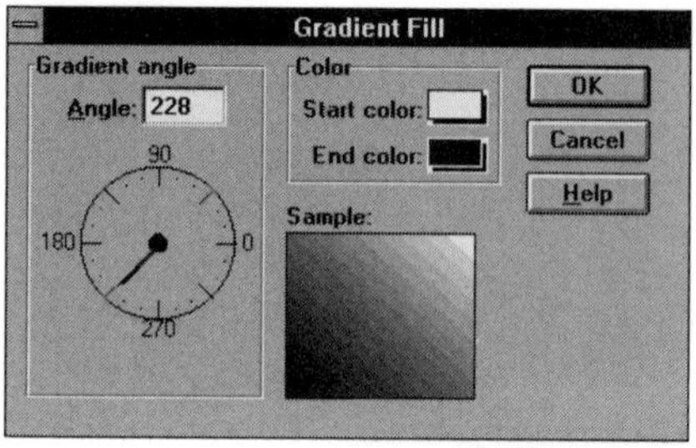


2. Click the Start color and End color boxes to select the colors that you want. You can mix custom colors the same way as you do in the Solid Color Fill dialog box.
3. Select the angle of the fill by typing a number in the Angle box or by dragging the indicator around the dial.
4. Click OK to apply your selections.

To use a bitmap image as a fill:

1. Choose Bitmap from the Background flyout menu to open the Bitmap Fill dialog box.

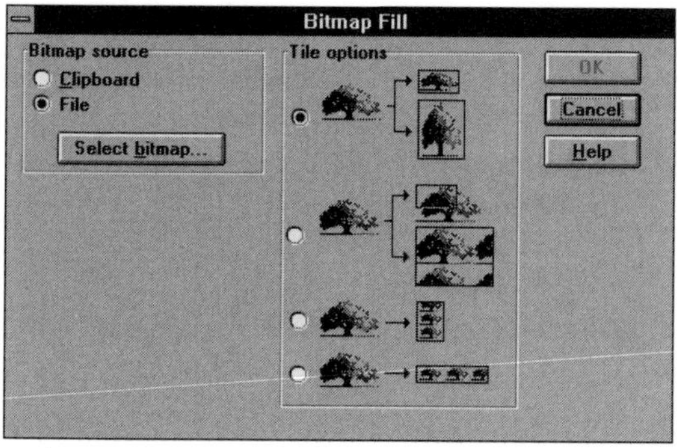


2. Choose the source for the image: either from the Clipboard or from a File. If you are importing from the Clipboard, skip to Step 6.

   TIP: If you want to import an image from the Clipboard, copy it to the Clipboard before opening the Bitmap Fill dialog box.

3. If you are importing an image from a File, click the Select bitmap button to open the Select Bitmap dialog box.

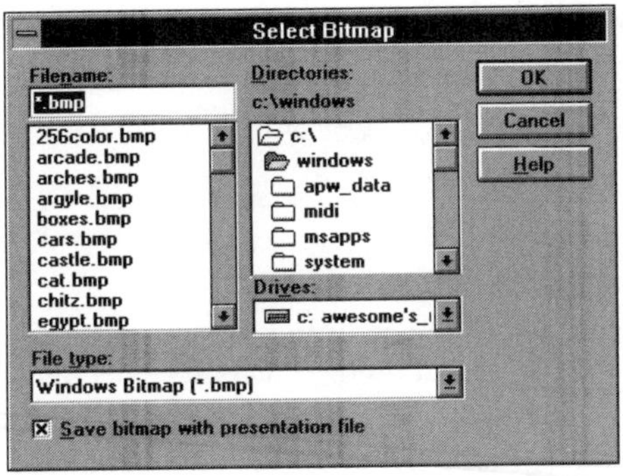


4. Select the file type from the File type drop-down list and the file from the Drives and Directories selection areas.
5. Click OK.
6. Select the Tile option you want in the Bitmap Fill dialog box.
7. Click OK.

To get real fancy and combine elements, use the Images command:

1. Choose Images from the Background flyout menu to open the Background Images dialog box.

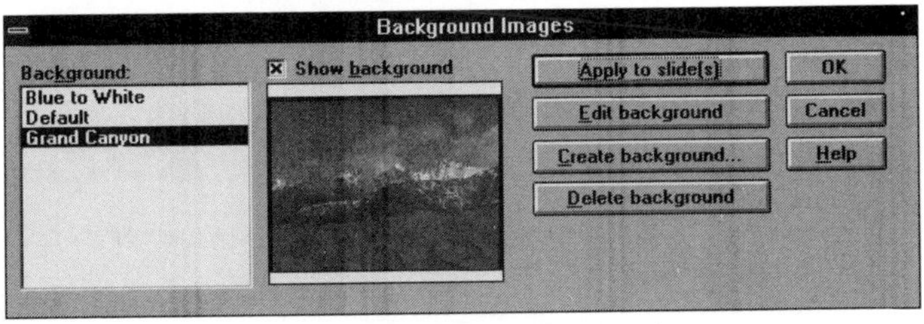


2. If you have already defined a background, you can select it from the Background list and click the Apply to slide(s) button.
3. Click OK to close the dialog box.

To create a new background:

1. Click the Create background button to open the Create Background dialog box.

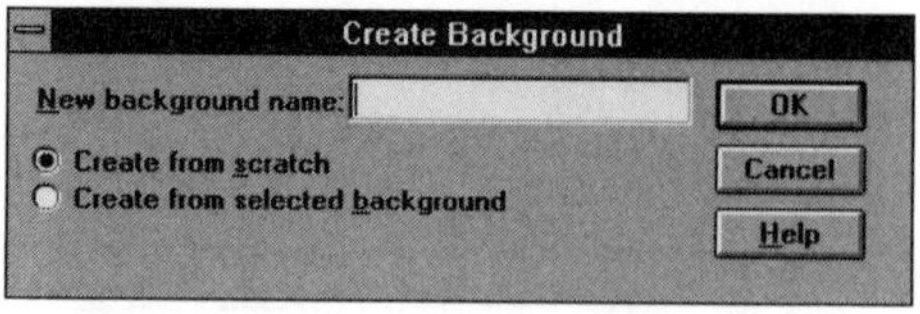


2. Designate the New background name.
3. Choose whether you want to create the background from scratch or base it on the currently selected background.
4. Click OK to close the dialog box and add the new name to the Background list in the Background Images dialog box.
5. Click the Edit background button to open a new window.
6. Make any changes you want.

   TIP: You can include images, objects with bitmap fills, lines — almost anything.
7. Click the Back to slide button in the status bar, the one down in the lower-right corner of the screen.
8. Go through the Style, Background, Images routine again to open the Background Images dialog box.
9. Select the name of your creation from the Background list.
10. Click the Apply to slide(s) button.
11. Click OK to close the dialog box.

## Cascade

Harvard Graphics allows you to have several presentations open at the same time. To avoid the shameful experience of an untidy screen, you may want to cascade all your pictures neatly, one on top of the other. The Cascade command does this automatically — and it's a lot easier than picking up your clothes.

### Digital rodent replacement

Shift + F5

## Using Cascade

If you have some deep-seated need to be neat, choose Cascade from the Windows menu to display all your open pictures, tidily stacked.

# Center on Slide

Another handy series of commands for the terminally neat. You can have Harvard Graphics automatically center selected objects on the slide horizontally, vertically, or both.

## Digital rodent replacement

Ctrl + H

Centers selected objects horizontally. No shortcut for vertical or both.

## Using Center on slide

1. Select the object(s) that you want to center. Shift+click to select more than one object at a time.
2. Choose Center on slide from the Graphics menu.
3. Choose Horizontally, Vertically, or Both from the menu that appears.

## More stuff

TIP

If a text box is wider than the text it contains, it won't center very well at all. To fix this problem, either center-justify the text in the box or drag the box handles to conform more closely to the length of the text.

# Change Chart Type

## From Gallery

## Chart types listed

Use this command to quickly change the type of chart or choose from the variations of the chart type.

## Using Change chart type

1. Select the chart you want to change.
2. Choose Change chart type from the Chart menu.

   TIP: The flyout menu does not let you select any chart type that cannot be used with the data in the current chart.
3. Select the type of chart you want to use from the flyout menu or choose From Gallery to open the Chart Gallery dialog box.
4. Select the chart and variation you want.
5. Click OK.

# Change Presentation Font

Changes the font used in the entire presentation. Does not affect point size or any other font attributes.

## Using Change presentation font

1. Choose Change presentation font from the Style menu to open the Change Presentation Font dialog box.

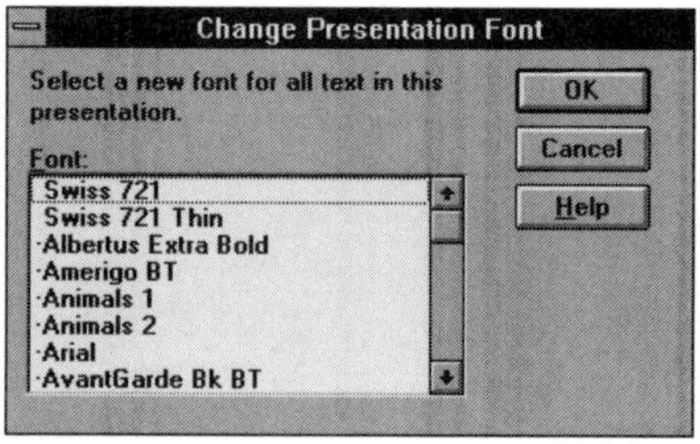

2. Select the new font from the scroll list.
3. Click OK.

## Chart Options

Each chart type can be modified in a bunch of ways. The following example uses a pie chart, but you use the same procedure to modify the options for any other type of chart.

### Digital rodent replacement

F8

### Using Chart options

1. Make the chart the visible slide in the Slide Editor.
2. Choose Chart options from the Chart menu to open the Chart Options dialog box.

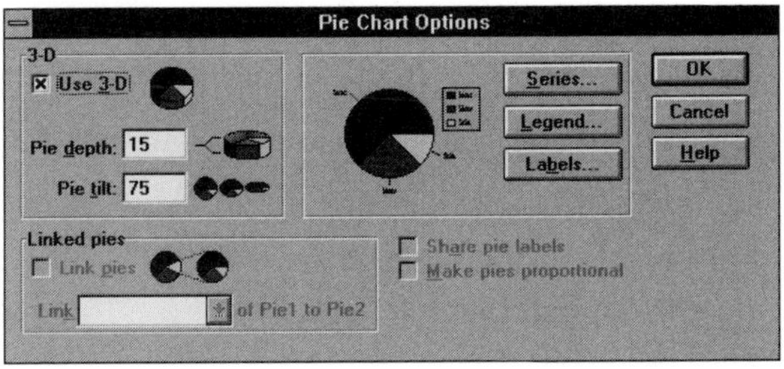


3. 3-D or not 3-D, that is the question. Whether 'tis nobler to be 3-D and set Depth and Tilt or not — and not.
4. Make any changes that you want to the other options. Each is linked to an extensive dialog box. Play and have fun.

TIP

Notice that when you point to the Series, Label, or Legend button in the pie chart example (other chart types may have other options), the representation of the chart changes to highlight the area of the chart that you can change by using the dialog box connected to the button.

# Chart to Image

Changes a chart to an image. Choosing this command breaks all links with any data, and the chart can no longer be changed or manipulated.

## Using Chart to image

1. Choose Chart to image from the Chart menu.
2. Answer Yes to the warning dialog box.

# Check Design

Choosing this command tells the Advisor, a white-haired and very wise, old silicon chip, to look at all the slides in your presentation and pester you if they don't conform to the rules emblazoned on its psyche.

## Using Check design

1. Open the presentation you want to check.
2. Choose Check design from the Edit menu to open the Check Design dialog box.

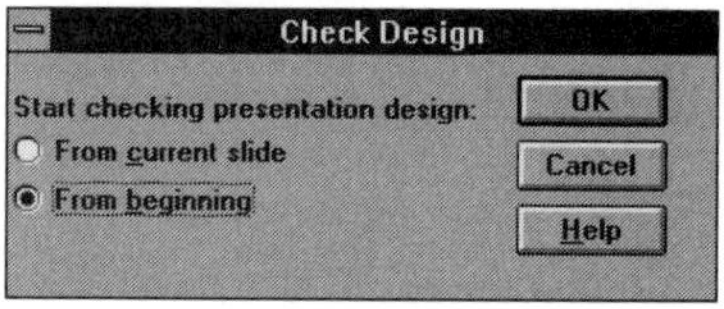


3. Click From current slide or From beginning.
4. Click OK.

   The Advisor opens and checks each slide against the rules provided by the aesthetics police. The checking process pauses at any slide that has a problem, and suggestions appear in the Check Design box of the Advisor.

5. To continue the check after a problem is discovered, click the Continue button in the Advisor Check Design box.

# Check Spelling

Nothing turns an audience hostile like a slide that has an *e* before an *i* without a *c* in view — unless the audience is really, really weird, that is. The danger icon is here only because so many of my students have added so many strange and wonderful spellings to dictionaries that the dictionary soon becomes of little use.

## Using Check spelling

1. Open the presentation you want to check.
2. Choose Check spelling from the Edit menu to open the Check Spelling dialog box.

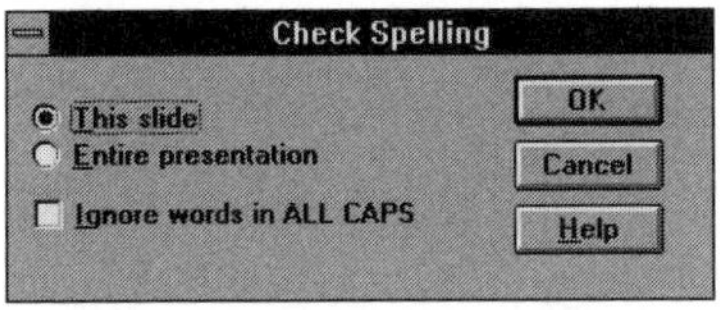


3. Click This slide or Entire presentation.
4. If you want the spelling checker to ignore words in all caps, select the Ignore words in ALL CAPS check box.
5. Click OK.

   The spelling checker whirls and rattles, and the Correct Spelling dialog box opens if it finds a questionable word.

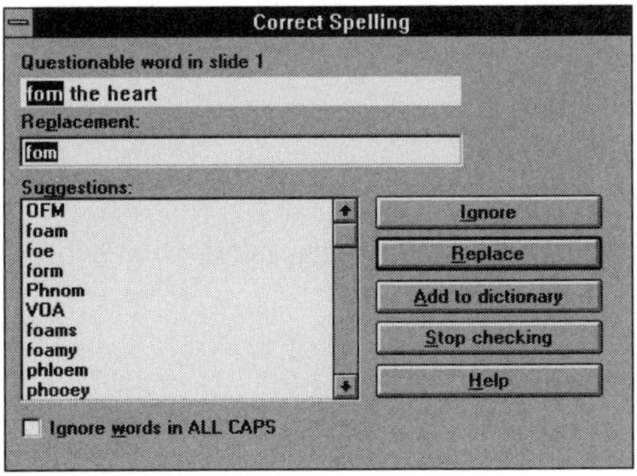

6. If the word is incorrect, type the proper spelling in the Replacement box or select the proper word from the Suggestions list.

   *or*

   If the word is correct, click the Ignore button to skip it or the Add to dictionary button to add the spelling to the dictionary.

## More stuff

TIP

Clicking the Add to dictionary button adds the word to the dictionary without giving you the opportunity to change your mind. If you make a mistake and add a misspelled word, you can edit the dictionary with a text editor — if you are very brave. The dictionary is called WINUSER.LEX and is located in the main HGW directory (or whatever directory you installed the program in). If you are in any doubt about this procedure, find a guru to do it for you. It's a lot easier to say, "He (or she) did it, not me!"

# Circular

The Circular command takes a selected text string and makes it follow a circular path.

## Using Circular

1. In the Slide Editor, select the text you want to modify.
2. Choose Circular from the Text menu.
3. To change the amount of arc of the text, drag any side selection handle in to increase the arc or out to flatten the arc.

## More stuff

The guidelines reflect the length of the text, which makes the process real easy.

## Clear

Removes the currently selected object from the slide.

### Digital rodent replacement

Del

### Using Clear

1. Select the object(s) you want to remove.
2. Choose Clear from the Edit menu.

## Close

Closes the current image and leaves Harvard Graphics active.

### Using Close

1. Choose Close from the File menu.
2. If you've made changes since your last save, Harvard Graphics asks you whether you want to save them. Answer Yes if you do.

## Collapse

Collapses an outline to show only topics. This command can also show all titles.

REFERENCE

See Outline for more information about this command.

## Color (Text Menu)

Changes the color of selected text.

## Using Color

1. Select the text that you want to change.
2. Choose Color from the Text menu to open the Text Color dialog box.

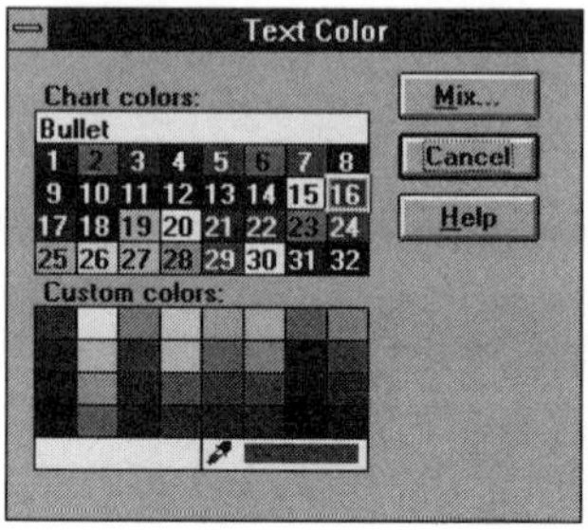


3. Click the color you want in the palette and then click OK, or click the Mix button to create a custom color in the Mix Custom Colors dialog box.

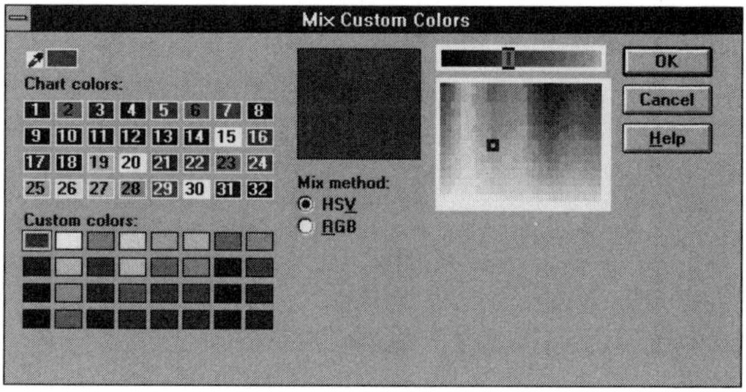


4. Drag the sliders until the color you want appears in the preview area. Then click OK to return to the Text Color dialog box.
5. The new color now appears in the Custom colors area. Click it to apply it to the text.

# Color Palette

## Select

## Save

## Edit

A color palette is a group of colors that have been designed to work well with each other. They are useful because many fancy and high-priced color monitors can display 16 million or so different hues, thereby giving people like me 8 million or so chances to come up with two that clash horribly.

## Using Color palette

To select one of the predesigned color coordinated palettes:

1. Choose Color palette from the Style menu.
2. Choose Select from the flyout menu to open the Select Color Palette dialog box.

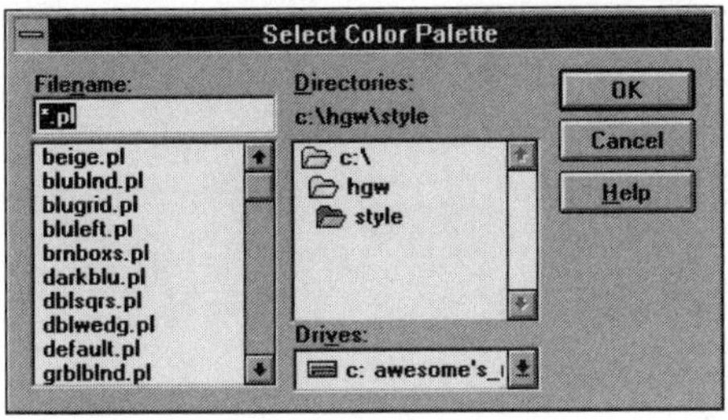


3. Double-click the palette you want.

   To see what each option looks like, open the presentation called PALETTE.PRS, which comes with Harvard Graphics. Each slide in the presentation gives an example of a color palette.

4. Click OK.

To edit an existing palette:

1. Choose Color palette from the Style menu.
2. Choose Edit from the flyout menu to open the Edit Color Palette dialog box.

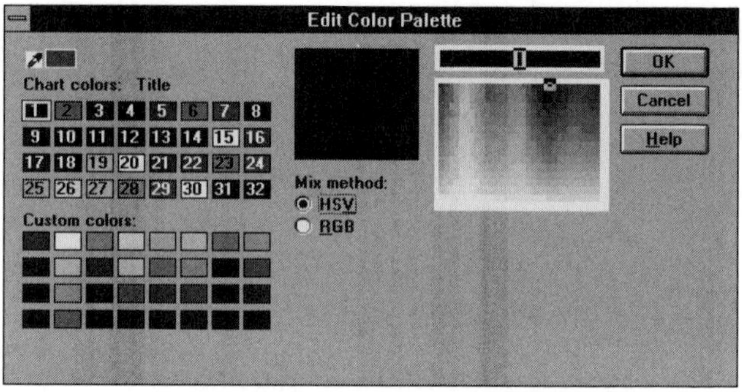


3. Click the number of the element that you want to change (see the following chart).
4. Slide the sliders around until the color you want shows up in the preview area.
5. Click OK.

To save a color palette after you mess with it:

1. Choose Color palette from the Style menu.
2. Choose Save from the flyout menu to open the Save Color Palette dialog box.

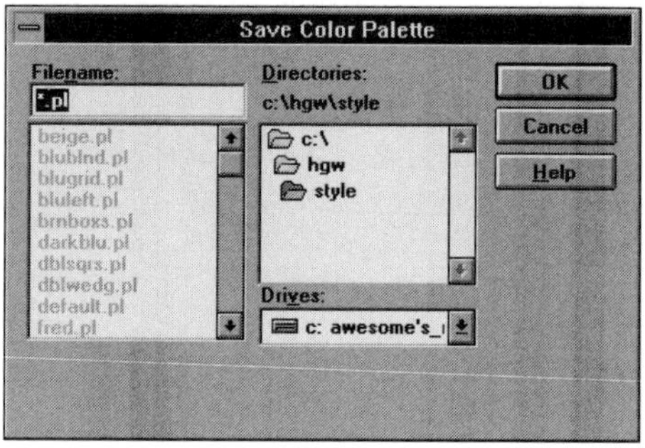


3. Give the new color palette a name.
4. Click OK.

## More stuff

To see the colors in the existing palette, click the solid fill button in the attribute bar.

| *Number* | *What It Means:* |
|---|---|
| 1 | Title |
| 2 | Subtitle 1 |
| 3 | Subtitle 2 |
| 4 | Text |
| 5 | Text high |
| 6 | Text dim |
| 7 | Footnote |
| 8 | X-axis label |
| 9 | Y1-axis label |
| 10 | Y2-axis label |
| 11 | X-axis title |
| 12 | Y1-axis title |
| 13 | Y2-axis title |
| 14 | Frame |
| 15 | Frame background |
| 16 | Bullet |
| 17 | Bullet dim |
| 18 | Lines |
| 19 | Shadow |
| 20 | Legend |
| 21 | Series 1 |
| 22 | Series 2 |
| 23 | Series 3 |
| 24 | Series 4 |
| 25 | Series 5 |
| 26 | Series 6 |
| 27 | Goal Y1 |
| 28 | Goal Y2 |
| 29 | Draw |
| 30 | Background 1 |
| 31 | Background 2 |
| 32 | Outlines |

## Conference, Conference Setup

As a matter of self-preservation, no ordinary presenter — especially an "outsider" — should even consider messing about with the network settings of someone else's equipment. If you want to display a presentation on many computers at the same time, get the LAN manager or network administrator to set everything up for you.

The commands are found under Conference setup from the Options menu and Conference under the File menu.

## Copy

Copying an object makes a duplicate of it and places the duplicate on the Windows Clipboard.

### Ribbon bar icon

### Digital rodent replacement

Ctrl + C

### Using Copy

1. Select the object to copy.
2. Choose Copy from the Edit menu.

### More stuff

After you copy the object to the Clipboard, you can paste it into most Windows applications simply by selecting Paste from the application's Edit menu.

# Customize Icon Bar

Harvard Graphics allows you to enhance the icon bar and add a pretty picture for just about any command in the program. If you find that you are doing the same task over and over and locating the command in the menus is taking too much time, add an icon for that task to the icon bar.

## Using Customize icon bar

To add a new icon for a Harvard Graphics command:

1. Choose Customize icon bar from the Options menu to open the Customize Icon Bar dialog box.

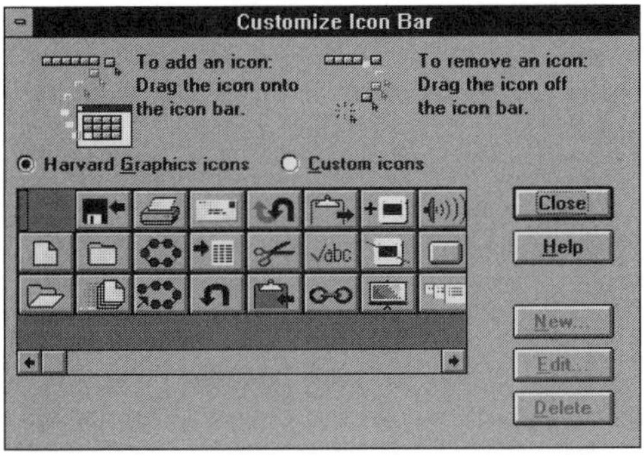


2. Click the Harvard Graphics icons radio button.
3. Find the icon that represents the command you want to add.

   TIP: A description of which command the icon performs appears in the bottom of the dialog box when you point to the icon.
4. Drag the icon from the dialog box onto the icon bar.
5. Click Close after you're finished.

To add an icon that starts another Windows application:

1. Choose Customize icon bar from the Options menu to open the Customize Icon Bar dialog box.
2. Click the Custom icons radio button.
3. Click the New button to open the Custom Icon dialog box.

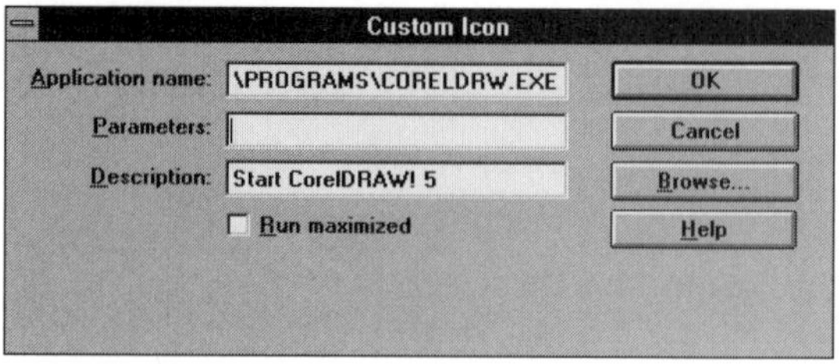


4. Fill in the Application name and path, any Parameters you want to use, and a Description that will appear in the Customize Icon Bar dialog box.

   TIP: Click the Browse button to open a directory tree that will help you find the program.

5. Select the Run maximized check box if you want the program to start full-screen. (If you don't check this box, the program starts up any old way it wants. It may be maximized, minimized, or between the two.)
6. Click OK to add the program's icon to the Customize Icon Bar dialog box.
7. Drag the icon from the dialog box onto the icon bar.
8. Click Close after you are finished.

## More stuff

TIP: You delete an icon from the icon bar in the same way, except you drag it *from* the icon bar when the Customize icon bar command is active.

# Cut

Cutting an object removes the object from the slide and places it on the Windows Clipboard.

## Ribbon bar icon

## Digital rodent replacement

Ctrl + X

## Using Cut

1. Select the object to cut.
2. Choose Cut from the Edit menu.

## More stuff

After you cut the object to the Clipboard, you can paste it into most Windows applications simply by choosing Paste from the application's Edit menu.

# DDE/OLE

Use this command to tell Harvard Graphics what to do with links and embedded objects.

## Using DDE/OLE

1. Choose DDE/OLE from the Options menu to open the DDE/OLE Options dialog box.

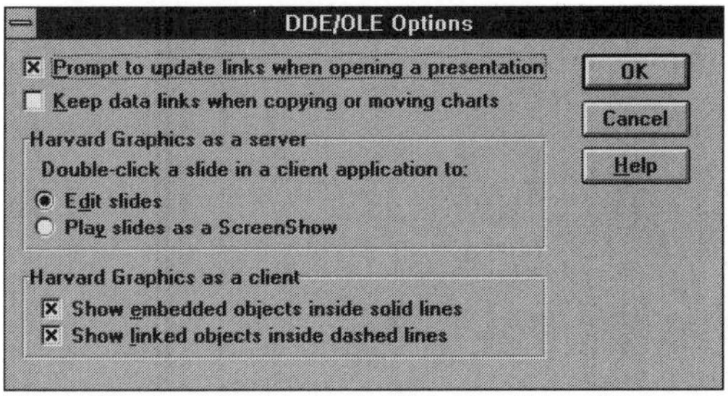


2. Select the following check boxes to do the following stuff:
   - **Prompt to update links when opening a presentation:** If you have linked an external source like a database to your presentation, select this check box to have Harvard Graphics check whether the source data has changed and, if so, update it.

- **Keep data links when copying or moving charts:** Place an X in this box if you want to maintain the link between a chart and an external data source even if you move the chart to another slide.
- **Harvard Graphics as a server:** These check boxes tell Harvard Graphics how to behave when one of its slides, or an entire slide show, is a linked object in another Windows application.

  **Edit slides:** Select this radio button if you want to be able to double-click a Harvard Graphics slide in another application, such as Word, and open Harvard Graphics to allow you to edit the slide.

  **Play slides as a ScreenShow:** Select this radio button if you want to be able to double-click a Harvard Graphics slide in another application, such as Word, and have the ScreenShow play.
- **Harvard Graphics as a client:** These two check boxes tell Harvard Graphics how to display objects that have been linked or embedded from other Windows applications.

  **Show embedded objects inside solid lines:** Objects that are embedded are surrounded by solid lines if this box is checked.

  **Show linked objects inside dashed lines:** Objects that are linked are surrounded by dashed lines if this box is checked.

# Defaults

Use this command to set some of the default options for Harvard Graphics.

## Using Defaults

1. Choose Defaults from the Options menu to open the Defaults dialog box.

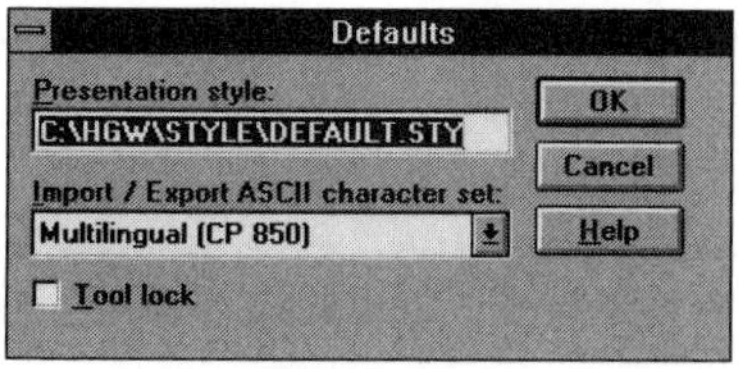


2. Modify the following items to change the default:
   - **Presentation style:** Insert the full DOS name (including the path) of the style you want to open as the default presentation style.
   - **Import/Export ASCII character set:** This drop-down list contains several options for languages to use when Harvard Graphics imports or exports ASCII text. Amaze your friends and use Portuguese (or if Portuguese is your native language, try using Nordic).
   - **Tool lock:** By default, whenever you finish using a tool, it becomes deselected and the selection tool becomes active. This default can be a real pain if you want to draw several lines or shapes. Placing an X in this check box keeps the last tool that you used active until you use another.

## More stuff

To set the default drives and directories, see the Paths command. To set the default view and measurement units, see the Display command.

# Delete Row/Column

Deletes the selected row or column from a Data Form. This command operates just like the Delete row and column commands in a typical spreadsheet.

## Using Delete row/column

1. Select the slide that you want to modify.
2. Choose Edit data slide from the Chart menu to open the chart's Data Form.
3. Make a cell active in the row or column you want to delete.

4. Choose Row or Column from the Delete flyout menu of the Data menu.

## Delete Slide

Deletes the selected slide from the presentation. Works in Slide Editor and Slide Sorter.

### Using Delete slide

1. Select the slide that you want to delete.
2. Choose Delete slide from the Slide menu.

   TIP You cannot delete the only slide in a presentation.

## Display

Changes the way Harvard Graphics initially opens, as well as the default measurement system.

### Using Display

1. Choose Display from the Options menu to open the Display Options dialog box.

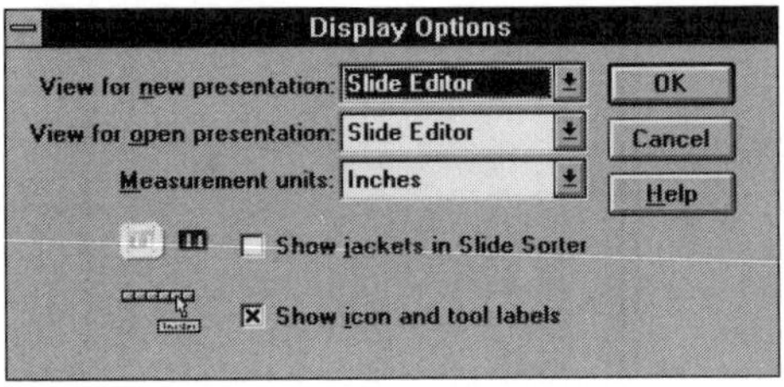


2. Change the following options to do the following stuff:
   - **View for new presentation:** Whenever you open a new presentation, you can have it automatically displayed in Outliner, Slide Sorter, or Slide Editor view.
   - **View for open presentation:** Whenever you open an existing presentation, you can have it automatically displayed in Outliner, Slide Sorter, or Slide Editor view.

- **Measurement units:** You have two choices: inches or centimeters. If you want picas or points, sorry.
- **Show jackets in Slide Sorter:** Put an X in this check box if you want each slide surrounded by a cute little picture of a slide jacket. You can't show nearly as many slides this way, but it looks kinda nifty.
- **Show icon and tool labels:** Put an X in this check box if you want Harvard Graphics to remind you what a tool or icon does. After you have used the program for a while, you probably will want to turn this option off.

## Edit Data

Use this command to edit or import data used on any slide.

### Using Edit data

To edit titles or cell contents:

1. Make the slide that contains the chart you want to edit active in either Slide Editor or Outliner.
2. Choose Edit data from the Chart menu to open the Data Form for the chart.

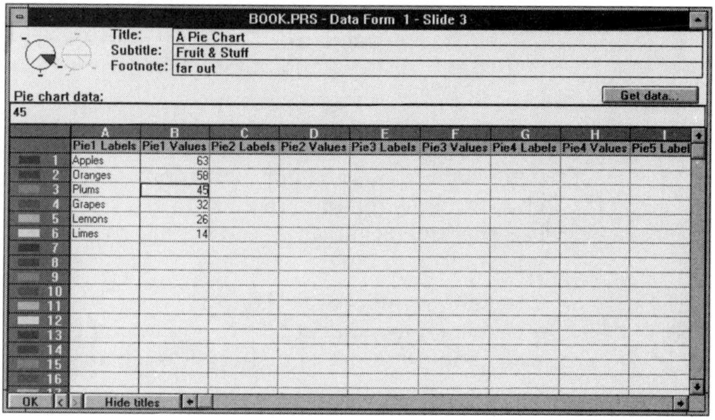


3. Edit the data in the titles or in the chart.

   TIP: To edit the data in the cell, it can be easier to select the cell and press Ctrl+E. This action moves the cursor to the editing line so that you can adjust the cell contents.

4. Click OK (lower-left corner of the dialog box) to accept the changes and return to the preceding view.

To import data:

1. Make the slide that contains the chart you want to edit active in either Slide Editor or Outliner.
2. Choose Edit data from the Chart menu to open the Data Form for the chart.
3. Click the Get data button to open the Import dialog box.

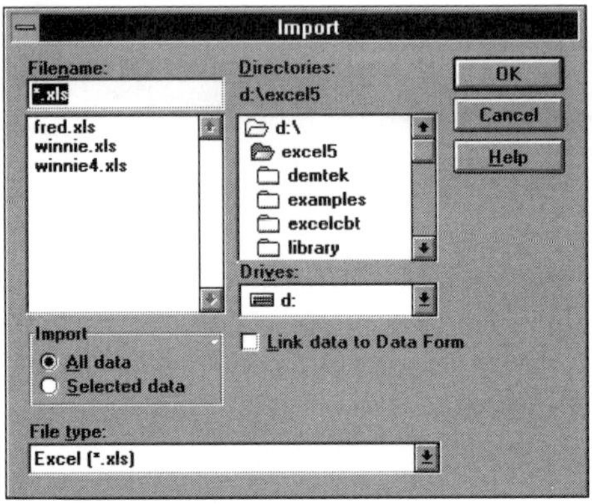


4. Select the type of file that you want from the File type drop-down list. You can import an Excel worksheet, a Lotus 1-2-3 worksheet, or a delimited ASCII file.

   If you want to import the entire worksheet, click the All data radio button.

   If you want to import only a portion of the spreadsheet, click the Selected data radio button. The Select Data dialog box that opens allows you to stipulate the range(s) of data you want to import.

   TIP

   You cannot import Excel 5 workbooks. Save the Excel file as a Version 4 worksheet before you attempt to import it. You also cannot import worksheets that incorporate charts.

5. Choose OK to import the data.

# Edit Handouts Master

Handouts are wonderful things to give your audience; they can reinforce a point or help an attendee recall what you said long after you go home. Handouts in Harvard Graphics are small representations of your slides, and their appearance is determined by the use of two commands: Presentation setup from the File menu and Edit handouts master from the Style menu.

## Using Edit handouts master

1. Choose Presentation setup from the File menu to open the Presentation Setup dialog box.

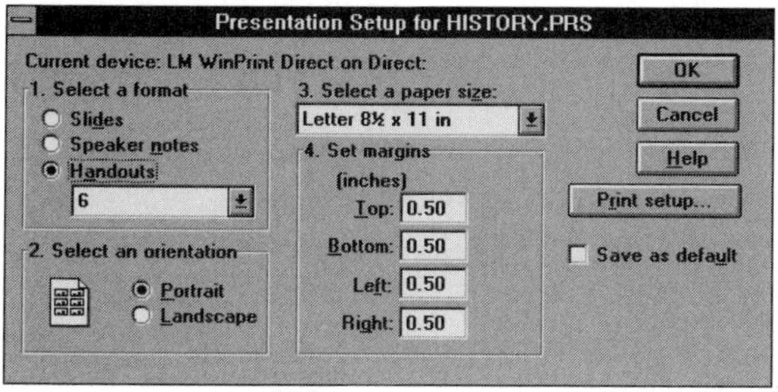


See Presentation Setup for a more complete description of the options in this dialog box.

2. Click the Print setup button to open the Print Setup dialog box.

See Print Setup to learn more about the options in this dialog box.

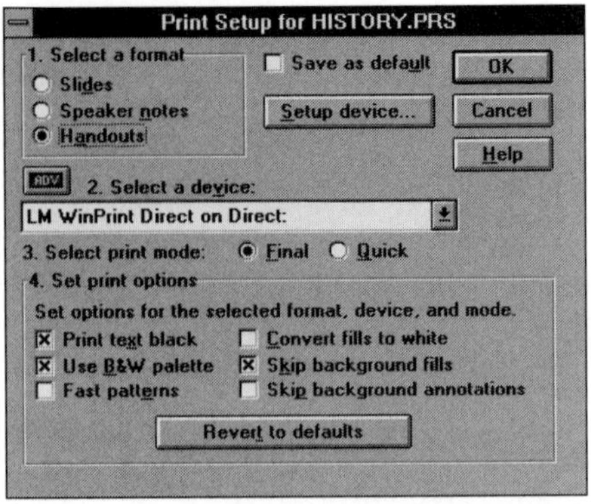


3. Click the Handouts radio button.
4. Select the printer you want from the list of installed printers in the Select a device drop-down list.
5. Select a print mode and any options you desire.
6. Click the OK button to close the Print Setup dialog box.
7. Click the Handouts radio button in the Presentation Setup dialog box. Select the number of slides that you want to print on each page and their position from the drop-down list.
8. Select the orientation and any other desired options in the remainder of the dialog box.

   See Presentation Setup for a discussion of the options.
9. Click OK to close the Presentation Setup dialog box.

   Now that the template is designed, you can actually do what the Edit handouts master command is designed to do.
10. Choose Edit handouts master from the Style menu to open the master template for handouts.
11. You can now change the appearance of frames, add borders, include text, and add special effects.

To add text to the handouts master:

1. Select the text tool.
2. Drag a text box with the text cursor where you want the text to appear.
3. Type away.

   Text that you place on the handouts master appears on each printout.

To change frames, add borders, or include symbols:

1. Select the frame(s) that you want to change in the handouts master by clicking or Shift-clicking them.
2. Choose Symbol Library from the Graphics menu to open the Open Symbol File dialog box.

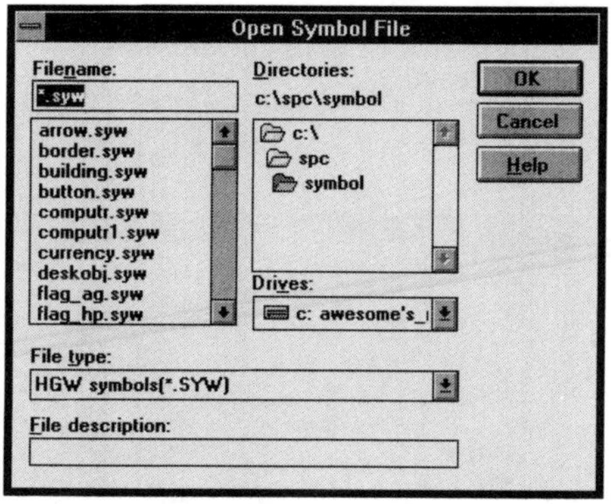


3. Double-click the name of the symbol library you want to use. This action opens the Symbol Library Manager with the symbol set displayed.

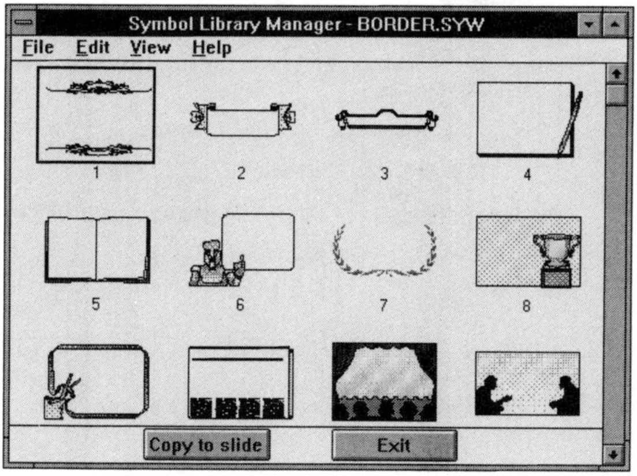

4. Select the symbol or border you want and click the Copy to slide button or drag it into the handouts master.
5. Paste the border as many times as you want.
6. Click Exit after you are finished.

To incorporate special effects:

1. Select the frame(s) that you want to change in the handouts master by clicking or Shift-clicking them.
2. Choose Special effects from the Graphics menu to open the Special Effects dialog box.

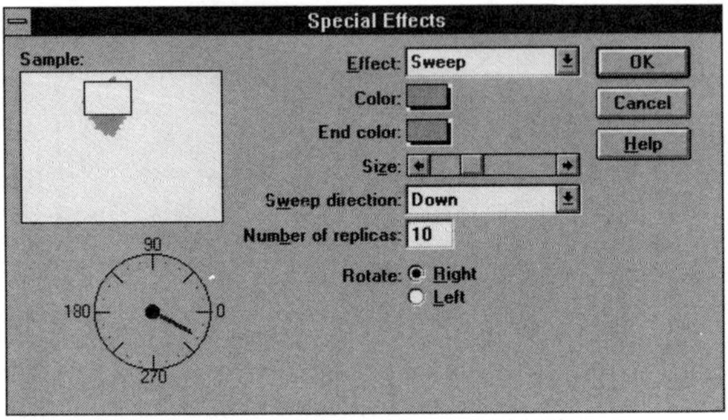


3. Choose the Effect you want:
   - **None:** Applies no special effect or removes whatever is there.
   - **Frame:** Changes the attributes of the frame (color, transparency, and size).
   - **Drop shadow:** Gives the impression of depth.
   - **Sweep:** Applies rotation and gives the appearance of movement to the frame.
4. Click OK to apply the effect.

See Special Effects for more information about the Special Effects dialog box.

## More stuff

Moving things about precisely can be hard when you drag them with the mouse. You do have the option of nudging shapes about with the arrow keys. Select the shape, in this case the border or symbol, and press the left, right, up, or down arrow to move the shape. When you have positioned the representation of the shape where you want it, press Enter to finalize the move.

# Edit Master Template

The master template establishes the parameters for the presentation. Changing settings here affects the placement of your titles, the colors that are available, and the placement of other graphic elements such as logos and stamps. What you change here appears on every slide of your presentation unless you specifically override the setting.

## Using Edit master template

1. Choose Edit master template from the Style menu.
2. Establish elements that you want to be on all slides of the presentation:
   - Move the position of titles by clicking the titles and dragging them to new locations.
   - Add a stamp.

     See Add Stamp for information about adding a date or slide number to all slides in a presentation.
   - Select the color palette you want to use for the entire presentation.

     See Color Palette for information about selecting a group of colors for a presentation.
   - Add a corporate logo or other graphic element to all slides in the presentation.

     See Import for information about bringing in data or graphics.
   - Apply special effects such as drop shadows to your titles.

     See Special Effects for information about doing special stuff to your slides.

- Select fills and line attributes.

  See Fills and Line Attributes for information about changing these elements.

## More stuff

Changes made to your presentation on the master template cannot be edited in the Slide Editor.

# Edit Object

Allows you to modify the shape of objects by dragging the object's control points to new locations.

## Digital rodent replacement

Ctrl + E

## Using Edit object

1. Select the object you want to modify.
2. Choose Edit object from the Graphics menu. The object appears with its control points visible.

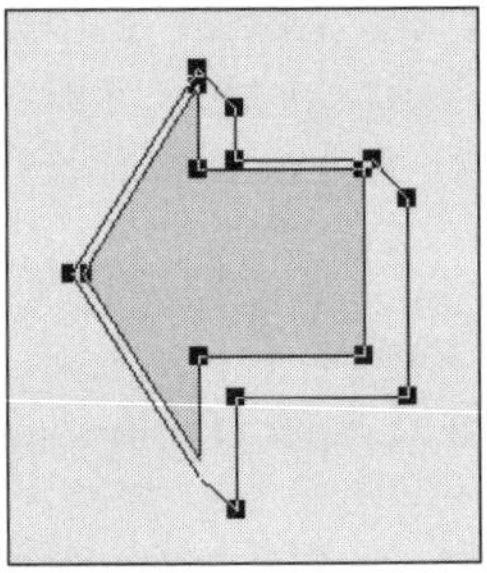

3. Position the cursor on any control point until it turns into a four-headed arrow, and then drag the control point to a new location.
4. Click the mouse button to return to the drawing.

## More stuff

You can modify the following objects:

- **Text:** Using Edit object places the selected text in a text box and allows you to edit content.
- **Squares and rectangles:** Edit object places one edit handle in the upper-left corner of the selected object. Moving this handle modifies the roundness of the object's corners.
- **Polygons, polylines, curves, and freehand drawings:** Control points are established wherever the shape changes direction; drag the control points hither and yon to change the object's shape.

# Edit ScreenShow Effects

Use this command to put the final touches on a presentation. You can set the opening and closing effects for each slide, add sound, set a length for a slide's display, establish branches in your presentation by using HyperShow links, and use Autobuild to construct a series of slides.

## Using Edit ScreenShow effects

1. Construct your presentation.
2. Choose Edit ScreenShow effects from the Slide menu to open the Edit ScreenShow Effects dialog box.

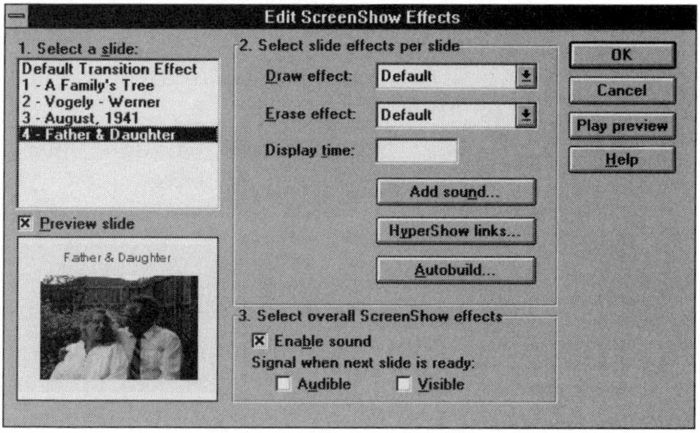

3. Select the slide that you want to change from the list of slides in the presentation.

   TIP: Slides are listed by their title and position in the show.

4. Click the Preview slide check box to see what you are doing.
5. Click the Draw effect drop-down list and choose any one of the 25 or so different ways for the chosen slide to be opened in the presentation.

   TIP: If you selected the Preview slide check box, you can see a representation of how the effect will look in the preview area.

6. Click the Erase effect drop-down list and choose any one of the 25 or so different ways for the chosen slide to be erased.
7. If you want the slide to show for a specified amount of time, enter it in the Display time box in minutes:seconds format. (2:05 displays the slide for two minutes, five seconds.)
8. Click the Add sound button to attach a sound file to the slide.

   REFERENCE: See Add Sound for an explanation of attaching sound to a slide.

9. To establish branches in the presentation, click the HyperShow links button.

   REFERENCE: See HyperShow Links to find out how to branch a presentation.

10. To display a slide as a series of its components, click the Autobuild button.

    REFERENCE: See Autobuild for a discussion of this feature.

11. Overall effects can be enabled in the Select overall ScreenShow effects area:
    - When checked, the Enable sound check box lets you play sound files in the presentation if your computer is set up to use the sound features of Windows 3.1 or later.
    - Check the Audible or Visible check boxes if you want a signal when the next slide is ready to view.
12. Click the Play preview button to see a preview of your entire presentation displayed in the preview area.
13. Click OK to exit the Edit ScreenShow Effects dialog box.

# Edit Speaker Notes

Speakers need notes about the same way that a trout needs worms. I mean, you can live without them, but the quality of life sure suffers. Speaker notes are small representations of the slides, with an area to include memory cues for those wonderful off-the-cuff remarks that you're famous for.

## Using Edit speaker notes

1. Select the slide that you want to annotate.
2. Choose Edit speaker notes from the Slide menu to open the editing screen.

3. Double-click in the Notes area and type the speaker notes you want.
4. Click the Back to slide button to return to the slide.

## More stuff

To print a copy of the speaker notes, choose Print from the File menu and select the Speaker notes radio button.

See Print for more information about printing various aspects of your presentation.

## Exit

Quits Harvard Graphics and returns you to wherever you started the program (to either the Windows Program Manager or the File Manager).

### Digital rodent replacement

Alt + F4

### More stuff

When you choose the Exit command from the File menu and have presentations open that have not been saved, a message dialog box appears and asks you whether you want to save your work. To save the stuff, choose Yes, and it is saved. If the presentation has not been saved previously, the Save As dialog box appears when you answer Yes. To abandon the changes, choose No.

## Expand

Expands an outline.

See Outline for more information about this command.

## Export . . .

Saves your presentation as text, chart, ScreenShow, or image files that you can use in another application. Export also saves a presentation to be used with the runtime player.

What you export depends on where you export it from:

- To export only the current slide, choose the Export command from Slide Editor view.

- To export an entire presentation, choose the Export command from Slide Sorter view.
- To export text as an ASCII file, choose the Export command from Outliner view.

## Using Export

1. Open the presentation and change to the view that lets you export the material you want.
2. Choose Export from the File menu to open the Export dialog box.

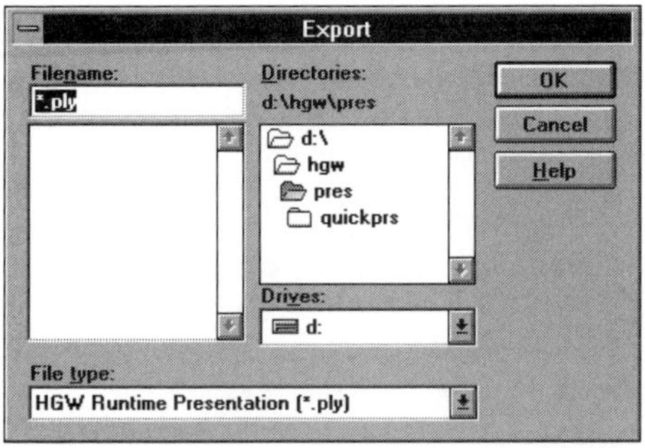


3. Give the file a name and select the type from the File type drop-down list.
4. Click OK.

## More stuff

- The File type list shows only the formats that are available in the current view.
- If you want to export only selected parts of a text file, select the text you want to export before choosing the Export command.
- If you are exporting a slide as a bitmap image, you see another dialog box, where you choose the options for format and resolution.

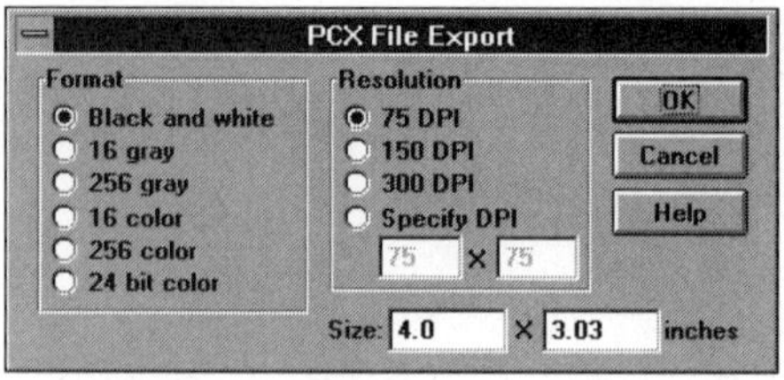


- When you are exporting an entire presentation as image files, each slide becomes a separate file. (Harvard Graphics limits the filename to five characters and adds a three-digit number to the filename to keep the images separate.)
- When you export an entire presentation to use with the runtime player, you see another dialog box, where you set the format for the presentation based on the capabilities of the computer that will show the presentation. If you are unsure of what to choose, select the least demanding format that will still show off your slides properly. VGA 16 color and VGA 256 color are both pretty basic and should display on the vast majority of computers.

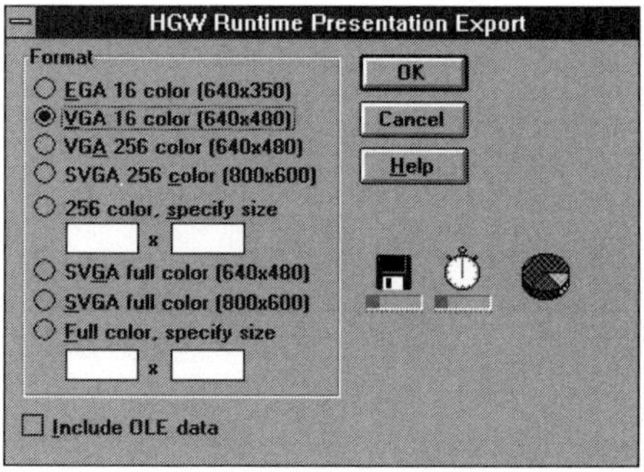


TIP: If you will be using the runtime player, be sure to copy it to a disk and take it with you or send it along with your show. The presentation player is called HGPLAYER.EXE and is located in the \SPC\PLAYER directory.

# Fill

## Solid

## Hatch / Pattern

## Gradient

## Bitmap

Use the Fill command to color an object.

## Using Fill

To fill an object with a uniform color, follow these steps:

1. Select the object.
2. Choose Solid from the Fill flyout menu in the Graphics menu to open the Solid Color Fill dialog box.

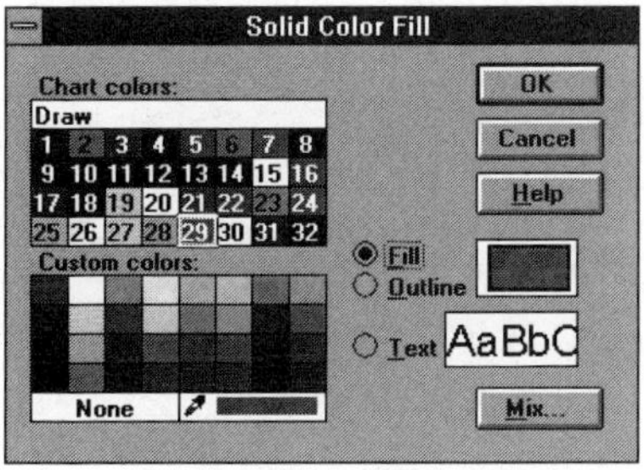


3. Select colors for the object Fill, Outline, and Text by clicking the corresponding radio button and then the color.

   The colors shown in the dialog box are the ones used in the current color palette. To change the palette, see Color Palette.
4. Click the Mix button to create a custom color, if you want.

To fill an object with a hatch or pattern fill, follow these steps:

1. Choose Hatch / Pattern from the Fill flyout menu in the Graphics menu to open the Hatch / Pattern Fill dialog box.

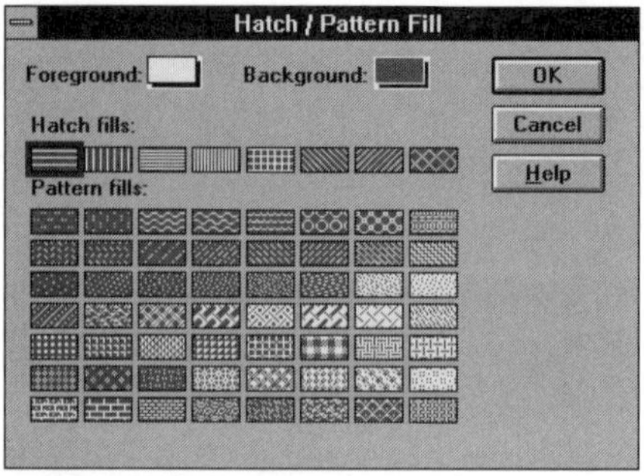


2. Click the Foreground and Background color boxes to select the colors that you want. You can mix custom colors the same way as in the Solid Color Fill dialog box, discussed earlier.
3. Click the Hatch or Pattern fill that you want.
4. Click OK to apply your selections.

For Gradient fills, follow these steps:

1. Choose Gradient from the Fill flyout menu in the Graphics menu to open the Gradient Fill dialog box.

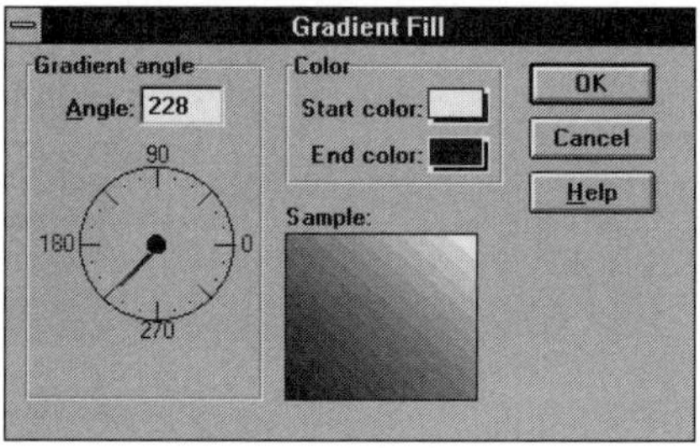


2. Click the Start and End color boxes to select the colors that you want. You can mix custom colors the same way as in the Solid Color Fill dialog box.
3. Select the angle of the fill by either typing a number in the Angle box or dragging the indicator around the dial.
4. Click OK to apply your selections.

To use a bitmap image as a fill, follow these steps:

1. Choose Bitmap from the Fill flyout menu in the Graphics menu to open the Bitmap Fill dialog box.

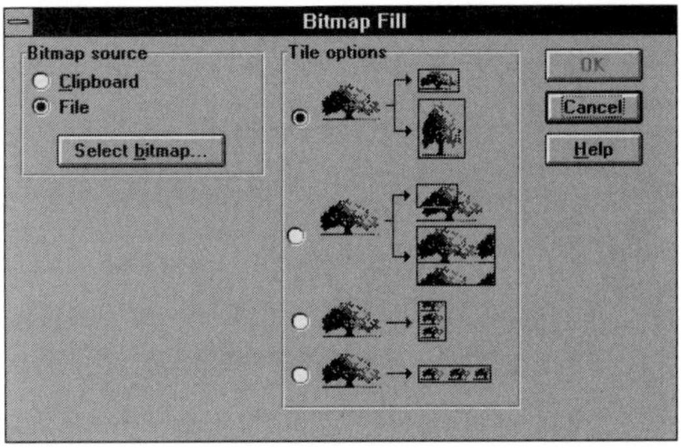


2. Choose the source for the image: either from the Clipboard or from a File. If you are importing from the Clipboard, skip to Step 6.

   TIP: If you want to import an image from the Clipboard, copy it to the Clipboard before opening the Bitmap Fill dialog box.

3. If you are importing an image from a file, click the Select bitmap button to open the Select Bitmap dialog box.

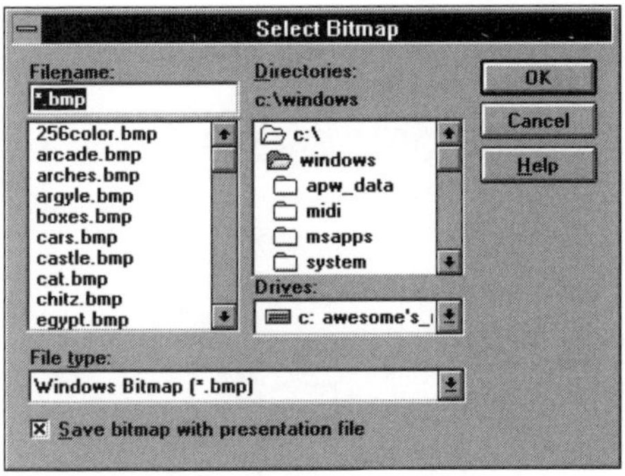


4. Select the file type from the File type drop-down list and the file from the Drives and Directories selection areas.
5. Choose OK.
6. Select the tile option you want in the Bitmap Fill dialog box.
7. Click OK.

# Flip

Flips the selected object end-for-end around its horizontal or vertical axis.

## Using Flip

1. Select the object(s).
2. Choose Horizontally or Vertically from the Flip flyout menu in the Graphics menu to turn the selected objects upside-down or backward.

# Font

Changes the font for any selected text.

## Using Font

1. Select the text that you want to change.
2. Choose Font from the Text menu to open the Select Font dialog box.

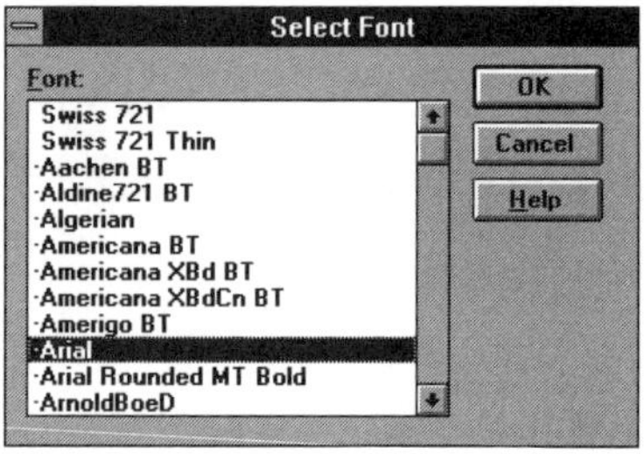


3. Click the Font you want in the scroll list.
4. Click OK.

## More stuff

You can change the default font for your presentation by using the Font command with no text selected.

To change other text attributes, see All Attributes.

# Frame

Use to select a frame for an XY chart. This command is also useful for a visual representation of goals.

## Using Frame

1. Make the XY chart active in the Slide Editor.
2. Choose Frame from the Chart menu to open the XY Chart Frame Options dialog box.

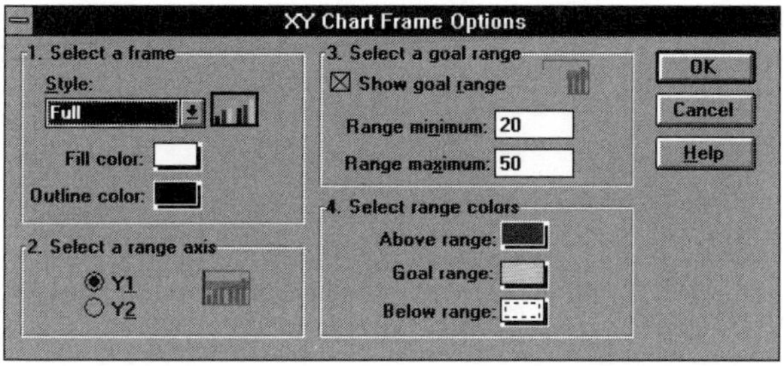


3. Select the type of frame that you want from the Style drop-down list.
   - **Full:** Displays a frame around the entire chart.
   - **XY:** Displays a frame on two sides (the X and Y axes).
   - **X only** or **Y only:** Uses the axis line as the frame.
   - **None:** Removes the frame.
4. Select Fill and Outline colors for the frame by clicking the appropriate box to open the Fill Color dialog box.

   See Color Palette to learn how to modify colors or find out what the numbers in the dialog box mean.
5. If you want your chart to have bands that separate certain numbers, such as colors representing levels of performance, click the Show goal range check box and enter Range minimum and Range maximum numbers.
6. Select the range colors you want to represent performance levels.
7. Click OK to complete the chart and apply the frame choices.

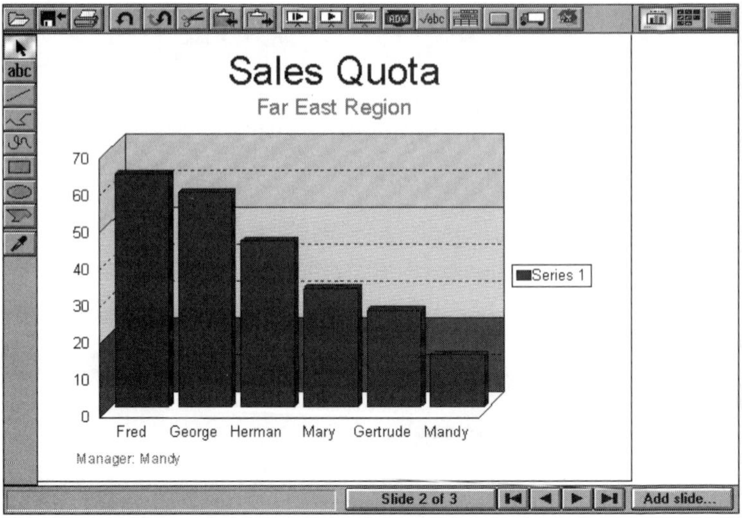


## Go to Slide

### Any

### First Home

### Previous PgUp

### Next PgDn

### Last End

Zip and whiz to a slide in your presentation.

### Digital rodent replacements

| *To Go Directly to, without Collecting $200* | *Press* |
|---|---|
| The first slide | Home |
| The preceding slide | PgUp |
| The next slide | PgDn |
| The last slide | End |

## Using Go to slide

If you don't want to go to any of the locations listed in the table, or you just want to be difficult to please:

1. Choose Any from the Go to slide flyout menu under the Slide menu to open the Go to Slide dialog box.

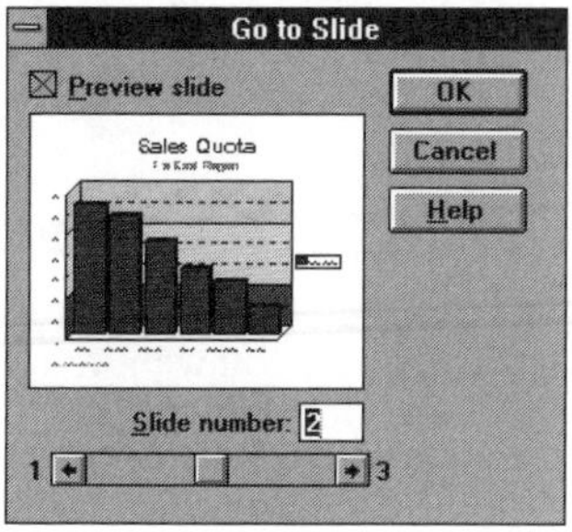


2. Check the Preview slide check box to activate the preview area.
3. Enter the Slide number you want to go to in the box, or click the arrows in the slider to find the one you want.
4. Click OK.

# Grid

Displays gridlines for XY and table charts and modifies the style of gridlines for XY charts.

## Using Grid

1. Choose Grid from the Chart menu.

   If your chart is a Table Chart, the Table Chart Grid Options dialog box opens.

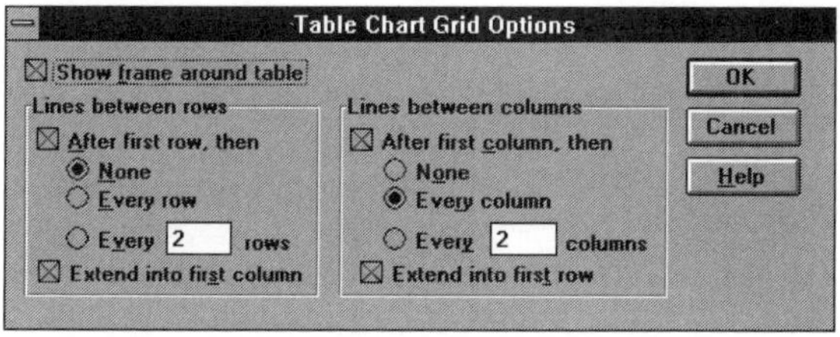

a. Select options for a frame around the table and lines between rows and columns.

b. If your chart is an XY Chart, the XY Chart Grid Options dialog box opens.

Otherwise, go to Step 2.

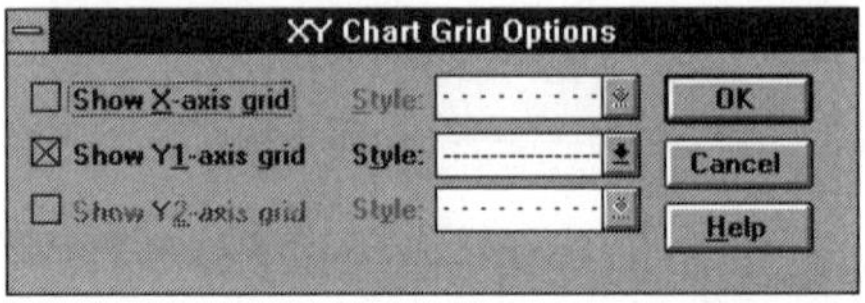


c. Check the gridlines that you want to show and select a line style from the drop-down list.

2. Click OK to apply the grid.

# Group

Groups all selected objects and allows them to be selected and modified as a single object.

## Digital rodent replacement

Ctrl + G

## Using Group

1. Select the objects that you want to group (Shift+click each object).
2. Choose Group from the Graphics menu.

## More stuff

You can select objects within a group without ungrouping them by clicking the object until selection handles appear around it.

## Hide Subtitle & Footnote

This command is found in the Outline menu. When active, it hides subtitles and footnotes in the presentation outline.

See Outline for more information about this command.

## HyperShow Links

HyperShows let your viewers control their own destinations. You can assign certain keys or buttons to let a viewer branch your presentation to another location, run an application, or even play a sound file.

### Using HyperShow links

1. Select the slide you want to be the starting point of your link in either the Slide Editor or Slide Sorter.
2. Choose HyperShow links from the Slide menu to open the Slide HyperShow Links dialog box.

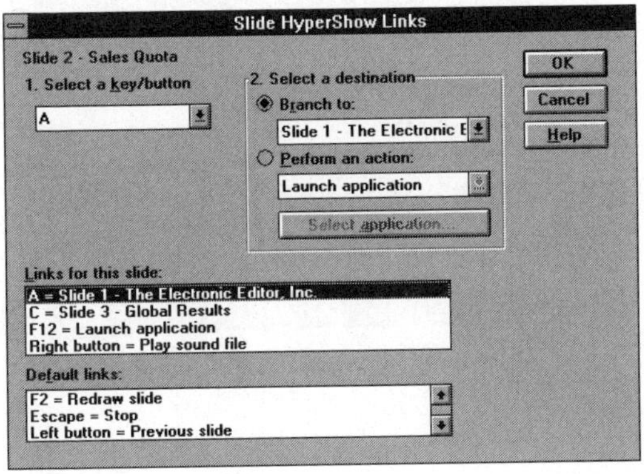


3. Select the key or button that the user should press to perform the action from the Select a key/button drop-down list.
4. In the Select a destination area:
   - If you want the key or button you selected in Step 3 to take the viewer to another slide, click the Branch to radio button and select the destination slide from the drop-down list.

TIP: The drop-down list contains the names used as titles for each slide, as well as generic destinations such as first, last, next, and so on.

- If you want the key or button you selected in Step 3 to perform an action, click the Perform an action radio button and select the type of action from the drop-down list. Then click the Select button to link the key to a particular program or file.

TIP: The Select button changes its name depending on the action selected.

5. Click OK to establish the HyperShow link.

### More stuff

REFERENCE: See Add/Edit HyperShow Button to add on-screen buttons that access HyperLinks.

TIP: Because HyperShow links, unlike HyperShow buttons, do not appear on-screen, be sure to include some text on the slide to tell the viewer what to press to do what or go where.

## Icon Bar

The icon bar is a great place to go when you want visual keys to specific commands. Nice as it is, there are times when you may prefer that it not hang around taking up valuable screen space. The Icon bar command takes it out of the neighborhood (makes it invisible) until you want it to come back.

### Using Icon bar

Choose Icon bar from the View menu to toggle the display of the bar on and off.

## Import

Imports spreadsheet or delimited ASCII data into the Data Form of a data or table chart; adds a graphic image to a slide; and imports ASCII text, charts, templates, and shows from Harvard Graphics for DOS.

What you import depends on where you import it to:

- Import into **Slide Editor** view:

  Harvard Graphics for DOS charts that will be added to Harvard Graphics for Windows slides

  Harvard Graphics for DOS shows

  Graphic images from other applications

- Import into **Slide Sorter** view:

  Harvard Graphics for DOS charts that will be added to existing presentations

- Import into **Outliner** view:

  ASCII text from other applications

## Using Import

1. Open the presentation and change to the view that lets you import the material you want.
2. Choose Import from the File menu to open the Import dialog box.

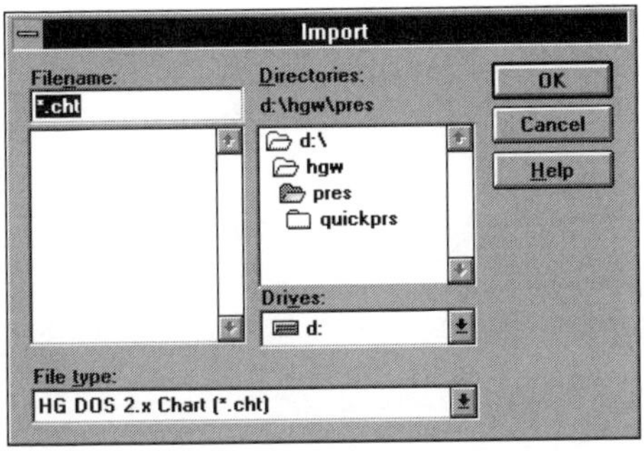


TIP: The dialog box changes with the view from which it is accessed. The File type list reflects only the types of files that can be imported into the current view.

3. Select the type from the File type drop-down list and the drive and directory that contain the file.
4. Click OK to import and return to the original view.

## More stuff

REFERENCE: See Edit Data for information about importing data into a Data Form.

# Indent

This command is found in the Outline menu. When selected, it indents the position in an organization chart one level.

## Digital rodent replacement

Tab

See Outline for more information about this command.

# Insert Embedded Object

Embedded objects become part of the Harvard Graphics slide. When you double-click an embedded object, you open the application in which the object was created, with the object displayed and ready for editing. When you return to Harvard Graphics, the slide reflects any changes you made to the object.

## Using Insert embedded object

1. Make the slide that is to contain the embedded object active in Slide Editor.
2. Choose Insert embedded object from the Edit menu to open the Insert Embedded Object dialog box.

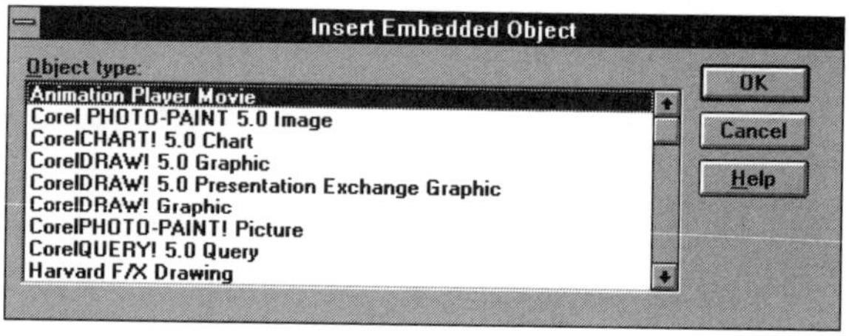


The applications that show in the Insert Embedded Object dialog box are those that have registered themselves with Windows. If you have Windows applications that do not appear in this list, find a guru who knows about the REGEDIT.EXE program. ***Warning:*** Before you mess with REGEDIT, be sure to back up a file called REG.DAT, just in case you blow it.

3. Select the application that you want to use to create the embedded object.
4. Click OK. Your computer whirls and chugs while it opens the requested application.
5. Create the object and select the command, usually Update and Return to, that closes the server application and returns to Harvard Graphics.

## More stuff

TIP

If you want to embed an object that you have already created, open the server application and copy the object to the Clipboard. Return to Harvard Graphics and choose the Paste command from the Edit menu.

Embedding the animations that came with Harvard Graphics is a little different. In Step 3, choose Animation player movie. Doing so opens the Animation Player-Movie dialog box.

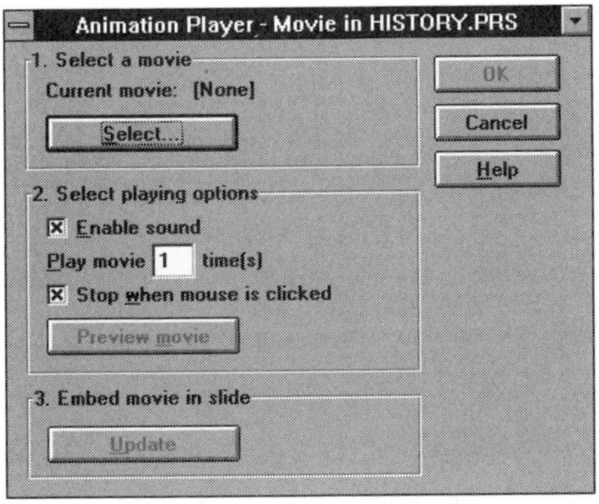


Click the Select button and choose a movie from the resulting dialog box. The Harvard Graphics movies are in the \SPC\ANIMATE directory. Click OK until you return to your slide. Double-clicking the movie's icon runs the movie.

You can add these movies to other Windows applications, too.

## Insert Row/Column

Inserts a row or column into a Data Form. This command operates just like the insert row and column commands in a typical spreadsheet.

## Using Insert row/column

1. Select the slide that you want to modify.
2. Choose Edit data slide from the Chart menu to open the chart's Data Form.
3. Make a cell active in the row or column to the right of, or immediately below, the place you want the new row or column inserted.
4. Choose Row or Column from the Insert flyout menu of the Data menu.

# Labels

Formats X- and Y-axis labels and shows data labels on charts.

## Using Labels

1. Choose Labels from the Chart menu to open the XY Chart Label Options dialog box.

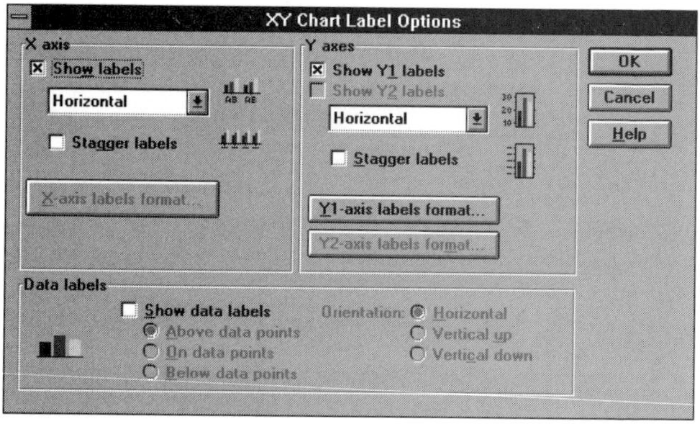


2. Select the options that you want:
   - X-axis group:

     **Show labels:** Toggles the display of X-axis labels.

     **Orientation:** Select the positioning and display of the X-axis labels.

     **Stagger labels:** If the labels are too long, selecting this check box staggers them.

**X-axis labels format:** Available only if X-axis labels are numeric. Sets the format of the numeric display.

- Y-axis group:

  **Show Y1 or Y2 labels:** Toggles the display of Y-axis labels.

  **Orientation:** Select the positioning and display of the Y-axis labels.

  **Stagger labels:** If the labels are too long, selecting this check box staggers them.

  **Y-axis labels format:** Available only if Y-axis labels are numeric. Sets the format of the numeric display.

- Data labels group:

  **Show data labels:** Shows values for the actual data points.

  **Label position and orientation buttons:** Select the position and orientation of the data labels.

# Legend

The legend is that cute little box that indicates what the colors mean. You use the Legend command to show or remove a legend, add or remove a legend title, set the location of the legend, and add a frame to the legend.

## Using Legend

1. Make the chart active in the Slide Editor.
2. Choose Legend from the Chart menu to open the Legend Options dialog box.

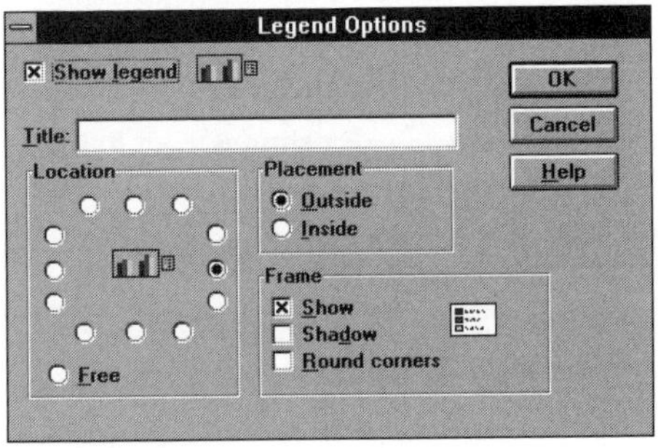

3. Select the Show legend check box to toggle the display of the legend on or off.
4. If you want the legend to have a title, enter it in the Title box.
5. Select the radio button that corresponds to the location where you want the legend placed, or select Free if you want to be able to drag the legend about on the slide.
6. Select Outside or Inside to place the legend outside the chart boundaries or within them.
7. Select the Frame attributes you want.
8. Click OK.

# Line Attributes

Sets the thickness, color, and style of lines.

## Using Line attributes

1. Select the object or line that you want to modify.
2. Choose Line attributes from the Graphics menu to open the Line Attributes dialog box.

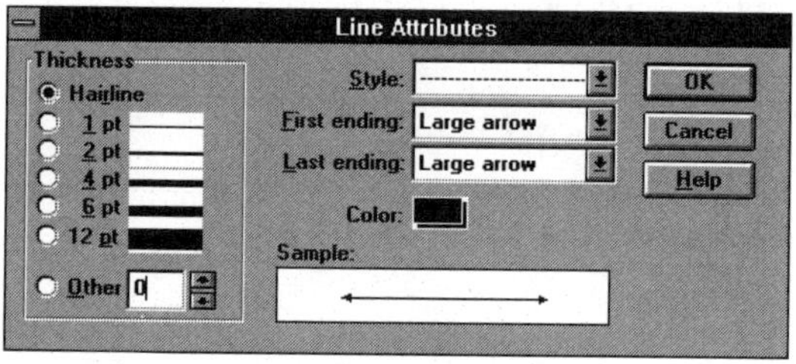


3. Select the desired line Thickness.
4. If the line thickness is Hairline, select a line style from the Style drop-down list.
5. Select one of the choices for line endings (None, Small arrow, or Large arrow).
6. Click the Color button to open the palette and choose another color for the line.
7. Click OK to make the changes and return to the slide.

## More stuff

TIP

To change the line attributes of any new lines (the default), follow the preceding steps with no objects or lines selected.

# Links . . .

Lets you view, update, or change links to other Windows applications (using OLE or DDE). This command is useful and worth your effort to learn. If your slide includes text generated in Word for Windows 6, for example, you can Paste Special it into Harvard Graphics and maintain a link between it and Word. When you update the text in Word, that text is updated in the slide. Links can be created between any Windows applications that are OLE- and DDE-aware.

## Links dialog box

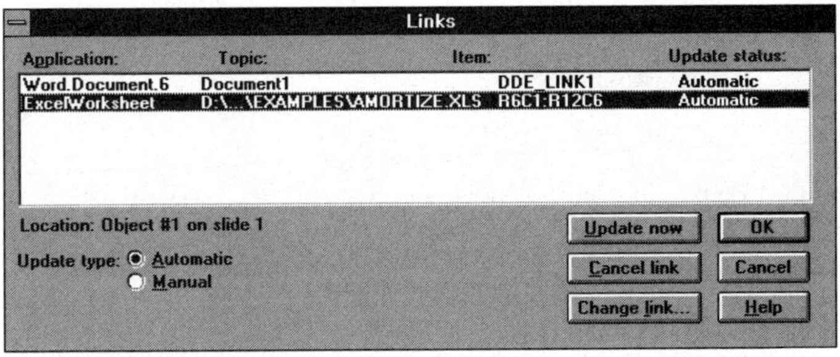


## Using Links

1. Choose Links from the Edit menu to open the Links dialog box.
2. Select the linked file that you want to change.
3. Make any of the following changes:
   - **Automatic:** Click the Automatic radio button to update the linked file anytime the file is changed in the source (server) application.
   - **Manual:** Click the Manual radio button to make the linked file update only when you select the Update now button.
   - **Cancel:** Click the Cancel button to close the dialog box.

- **Update now:** Click the Update now button to update manually linked files and objects.
- **Change link:** Click the Change link button to associate the object with a new application.
- **Cancel link:** Click the Cancel link button to terminate the linkage between the object and the source application.

## More stuff

WARNING!

Double-clicking a linked object opens the parent application with the linked file active and ready for edit. This is a really great feature of OLE, but be sure that you check the amount of free resources your computer has. (Look under About Program Manager in the Help menu of the Program Manager to see your system's statistics.) If your system resources are hovering around 35 percent or so, you may be risking a system lockup if you proceed to open yet another application.

You can insert linked objects into a Harvard Graphics slide in two ways: copy the object to the Clipboard and paste it into a slide or use the Insert embedded object command, discussed earlier, in the Edit menu.

# Move to Back

Places the selected object behind all other objects in the slide.

## Using Move to back

1. Select the object that you want to move.
2. Choose Move to back from the Graphics menu.

# Move to Front

Places the selected object in front of all other objects in the slide.

## Using Move to front

1. Select the object that you want to move.
2. Choose Move to front from the Graphics menu.

# New Presentation

Opens a new presentation.

## Digital rodent replacement

Ctrl + N

## Using New presentation

1. Choose New presentation from the File menu to open the New Presentation dialog box.

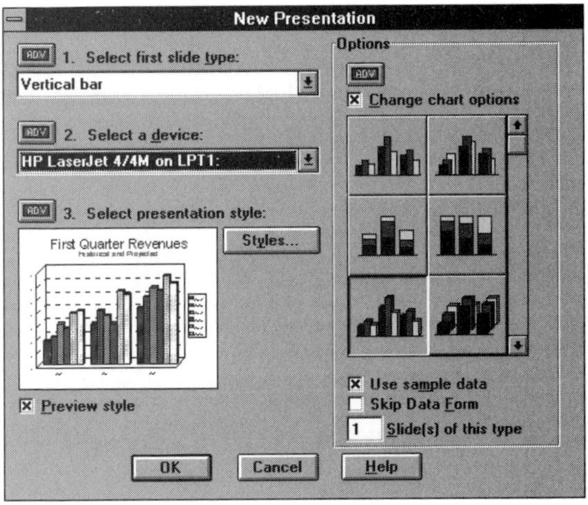


2. Select the first slide's Type, Device, and presentation Style.
3. Check Change chart options to select a different form from the chart options scroll list, if desired.
4. Check the Use sample data check box if you want a Data Form or chart constructed with sample information.
5. Check the Skip Data Form box to suppress the display of a Data Form.
6. Enter the number of slides of the selected type that you want created in the Slide(s) of this type box.
7. Click OK.

## More stuff

Click the ADV button anywhere along the way to get help and advice from that wise old silicon sage, the Advisor.

# Object

## Play

## Edit

## ScreenShow options

The Object command in the Edit menu changes its name and available options with the type of embedded object that is selected when you invoke the command. You use it to preview (or "prehear") objects that play, such as sound files, animations, and movies; to edit embedded objects in the server applications; and to set ScreenShow options.

## Using Object

1. Select the embedded object with the selection tool.
2. Choose the Object command from the Edit menu.

   TIP: The flyout menu can contain as many as three options: Play, Edit, and ScreenShow options. If the embedded object is not one that plays, such as a movie or a sound, the play option does not appear on the flyout menu.
3. Do one of the following from the flyout menu:
   - If the object is playable, choose Play to preview the animation, movie, or sound.
   - Choose Edit to open either the server application or the selection dialog box to change the embedded object.
   - Choose ScreenShow options to open the ScreenShow Options dialog box.

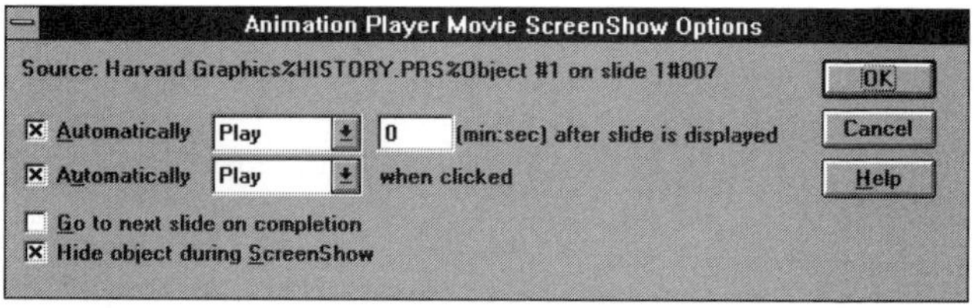

To have the object automatically play (or edit, or whatever else the selected embedded object likes to do) a predetermined amount of time after the slide opens, check the first Automatically check box, choose Play (or whatever) from the upper drop-down list, and insert the desired time (minutes:seconds) in the Time box.

To have the object play (or just do its thing) when you click it, check the second Automatically check box and choose Play (or whatever) from the lower drop-down list.

Select the Go to next slide on completion check box to have the ScreenShow open the next slide as soon as the embedded object is finished doing its thing.

Selecting the Hide object during ScreenShow check box keeps the embedded object's icon hidden while the show is showing.

4. Click OK to return to the slide.

# Open

Loads a presentation into Harvard Graphics.

## Toolbar icon

## Digital rodent replacement

Ctrl + O

## Using Open drawing

1. Choose Open from the File menu to access the Open dialog box.
2. Enter the filename in the Filename box or use the Drives and Directories boxes to locate the presentation.
3. If you want to open a copy of the presentation, leaving the original unchanged, check the Open a copy check box.

4. If you want to open the original presentation but not allow it to be changed, select the Open for read only check box.
5. Click OK.

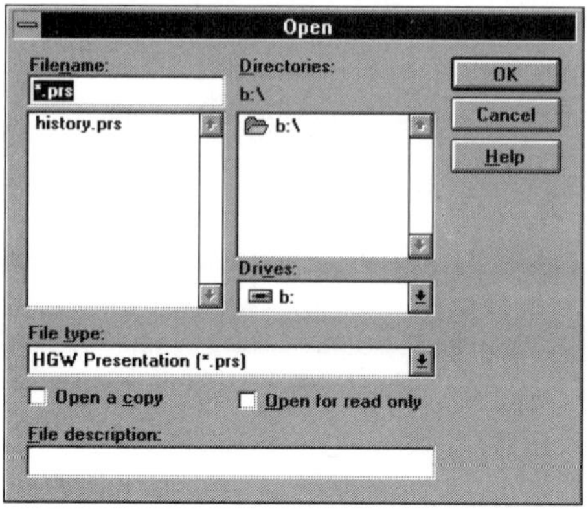


## More stuff

TIP

You can use wildcards in the Filename box. For example, entering *ex**.* shows a list of all files beginning with *ex* in the selected directory.

REFERENCE

See Save, Save As for more information about files and presentations.

# Organization Charts

What self-respecting baby boomer doesn't construct organization charts with his or her name prominently displayed right up there at the top? It's easy to do in Outliner view or on a Data Form with Harvard Graphics. You can even keep giving yourself promotions, as long as you can think of titles worthy of your name.

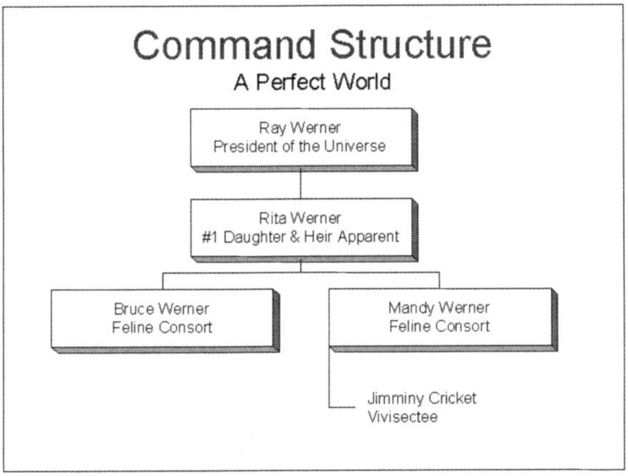


## Using Organization charts

1. Choose Add Slide from the Slide menu to open the Add Slide dialog box.

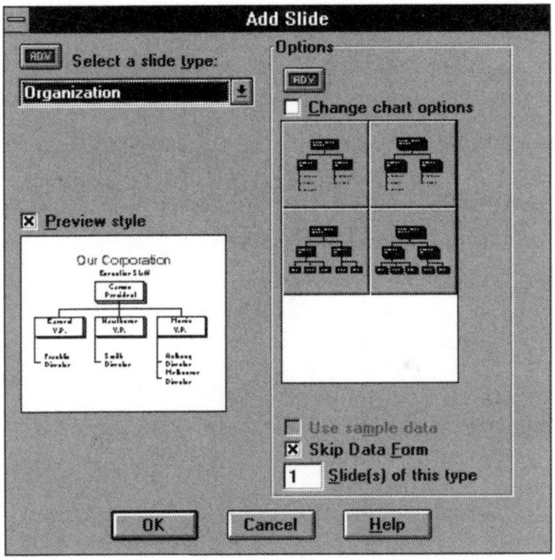


2. Choose Organization from the Select a slide type drop-down list.
3. Deselect the Skip Data Form check box.
4. Click OK to open the Data Form for your organization chart.

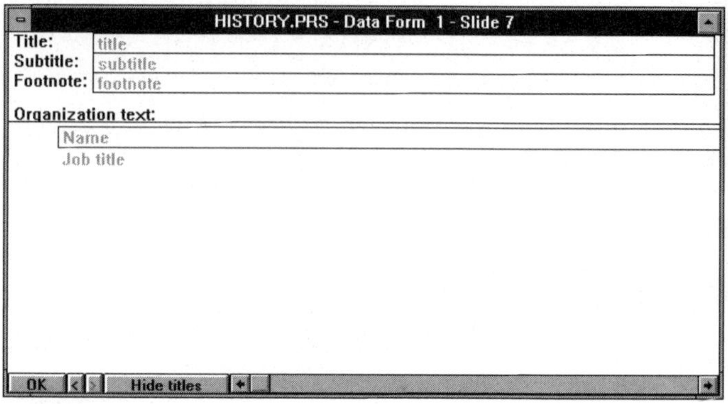


5. Fill in the information. Press Tab or Shift+Tab to promote and demote positions.

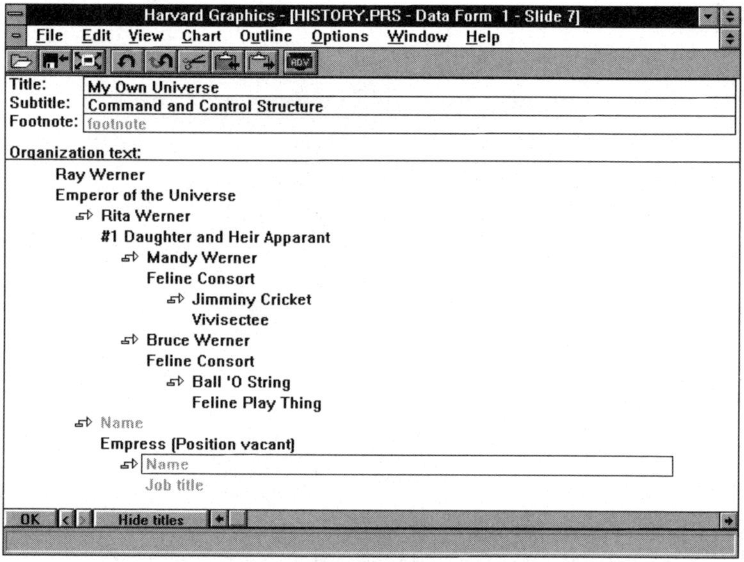


6. Click OK to finish the chart.

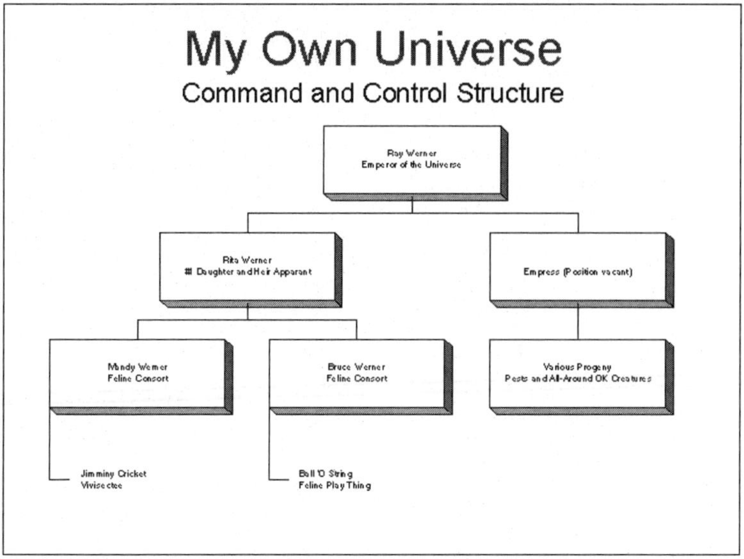


## More stuff

To move a position, open the Outliner view and drag the position's icon to a new location.

To move a group of positions, open the Outliner view and select the positions by dragging over them and then drag any icon in the selected group to the new location.

To change the style of the boxes, select the organization chart in the Slide Editor and then click the right mouse button. Select the style you want and then click OK.

TIP To change a bullet chart to an organization chart, click any bullet in the Outliner and choose Change Chart Type/Organization from the Chart menu.

# Outliner

One of the three possible on-screen views.

## Toolbar icon

# Using Outliner

Choose Outliner from the View menu to open an outline view of your presentation.

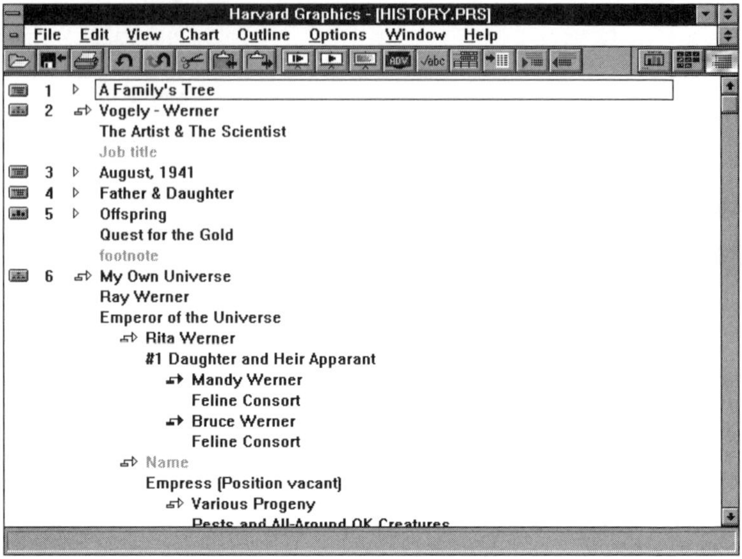


# More stuff

When the Outliner view is active, the outline can be manipulated through the Outline menu. This menu allows you to do the following:

- Collapse only the selected Topics or collapse All (the entire outline) to titles.
- Expand the menu to show only all in the selected Topic, or Expand all (the entire outline).
- Show subtitle & footnote.
- Hide subtitle & footnote.
- Indent position one level.
- Unindent position one level.
- Make slide summary. (Create a series of slides. Each first-level topic becomes a separate slide.)
- Remove slide summary.

- Change topic to Slide title.
- Change topic to Bullet item.

# Paste

Pastes Clipboard contents into a slide.

## Ribbon bar icon

## Digital rodent replacement

Ctrl + V

## Using Paste

1. Be sure that the object you want to paste into your slide is on the Clipboard.
2. Choose Paste from the Edit menu.

# Paste Special . . .

Pastes Clipboard contents into a slide and allows you to specify the format of the information and create a link to the source file.

## Paste Special dialog box

## Using Paste special

1. Be sure that the information you want to paste is on the Clipboard.
2. Choose Paste special from the Edit menu. This action opens the Paste Special dialog box.
3. Make selections in the dialog box:

   - The **Source** area displays the name and location of the source file providing the information.
   - Clicking the **Paste** button inserts the contents of the Clipboard into the drawing without creating a link to the source file.
   - Clicking **Paste link** inserts the contents of the Clipboard and creates a link to the source file.

     TIP

     The Paste link option is available only if the Clipboard contents came from an application that can link information to Harvard Graphics.
   - The **Data type** list area lets you choose which format you want to use. Several programs allow you to use differing formats of information, like RTF or ASCII.

# Paths

Changes the default drive and directories for files used by Harvard Graphics.

## Using Paths

1. Choose Paths from the Options menu to open the Paths dialog box.

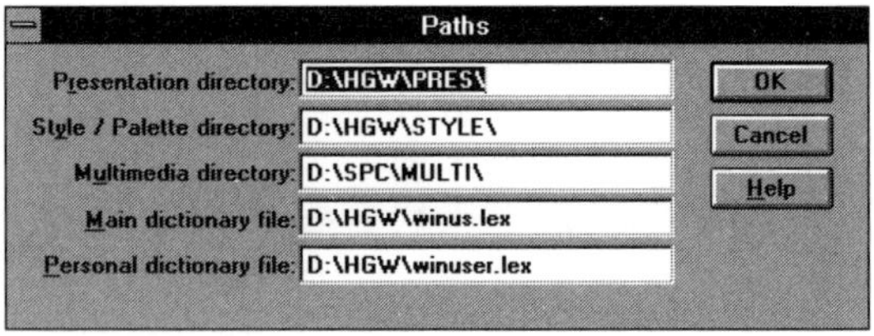

2. Fill in the locations of the files:
   - **Presentation directory:** Location for Harvard Graphics to store or look for presentations.
   - **Style / Palette directory:** Location for Harvard Graphics to store or look for styles and palettes.
   - **Multimedia directory:** Location of MID and WAV (sound) files.
   - **Main and Personal dictionary files:** Locations of the dictionaries. Entries have to be in these areas for Harvard Graphics to be able to check spelling.
3. Click OK to accept changes and return to the main program.

# Personal Dictionary

Adds, deletes, or changes words in your personal dictionary.

## Using Personal dictionary

To change the words in your personal dictionary:

1. Choose Personal dictionary from the Edit menu to open the Personal Dictionary dialog box.

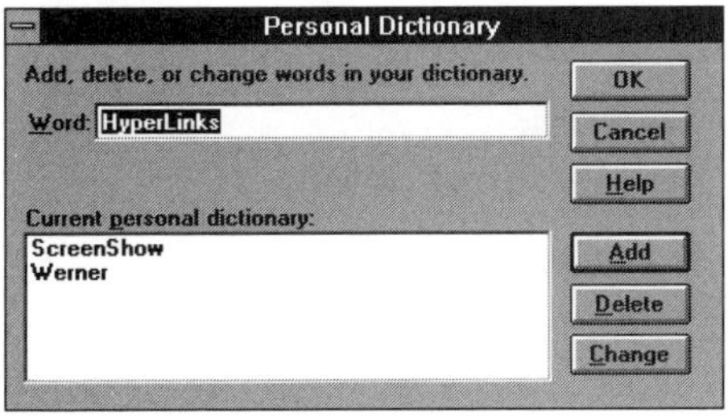


2. Perform the action that you want:
   - To add a new word, type it in the Word box and press the Add button.
   - To change a word, click it in the Current personal dictionary list to bring the word into the Word area, modify the word, and click the Change button.

- To delete a word from the personal dictionary, click it in the Current personal dictionary list to bring the word into the Word area and click the Delete button.

3. Click OK to close the Personal Dictionary dialog box.

## More stuff

See Paths for information about setting the location of your personal dictionary.

# Presentation Setup

Selects the print device, format, orientation, paper size, and margins.

## Using Presentation setup

1. Choose Presentation setup from the File menu to open the Presentation Setup dialog box.

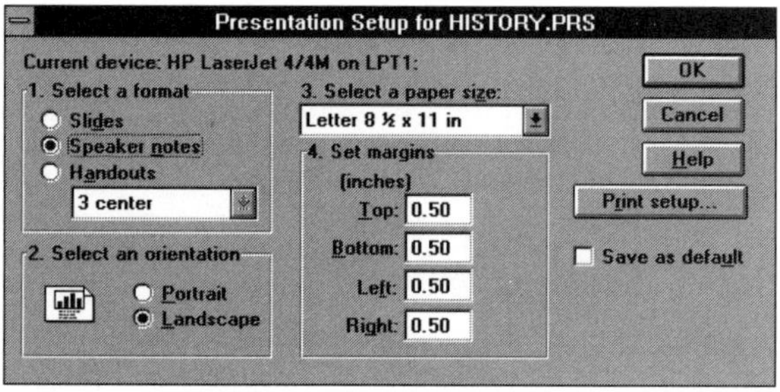


2. Click the Print setup button to select the printer and print-related options.

   See Print Setup for a discussion of the options in the Print Setup dialog box.

3. Select the format that you want to set up:
   - **Slides:** The only option available is print setup.
   - **Speaker notes:** Select the paper orientation, paper size, and margins you want.
   - **Handouts:** Select a layout option from the drop-down list, paper orientation, and margins.

4. If you want to save these settings as the default for all other presentations, check the Save as default check box.
5. Click the OK button to save the settings and close the Presentation Setup dialog box.

# Preview Slide

Lets you view a slide as it will appear in a show.

## Digital rodent replacement

F2

## Using Preview slide

1. Make the slide that you want to see active in the Slide Editor.
2. Choose Preview slide from the View menu.
3. Press any key to return to the program.

# Print

Lets you print all or part of your show, speaker notes, and handouts.

## Ribbon bar icon

## Digital rodent replacement

Ctrl + P

## Print dialog box

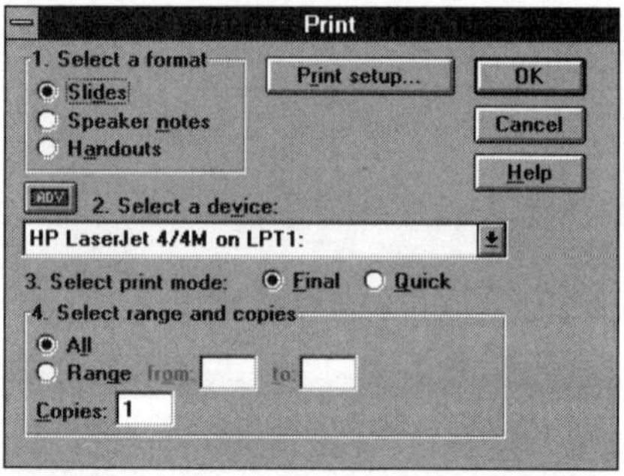


## Using Print

1. Choose Print from the File menu.
2. Select the item that you want to print: Slides, Speaker notes, or Handouts.
3. Select the device that you want to use for printing from the Select a device drop-down list.

   TIP

   You do not have to choose the same device for Slides, Speaker notes, and Handouts. You may want to send the slides out to a service bureau and therefore print them to a file using some high-end color printer's settings.

   Your service bureau can help you out here.
4. Select the print mode: Final for the best possible looking stuff or Quick for those of you who are less patient.
5. Select the desired range of pages:
   - **All:** Select this option to print the whole banana.
   - **Range:** Specify the range of pages you want to print.
6. Select the desired number of Copies.

# Print Setup

Selects print devices and options for printing.

## Print Setup dialog box

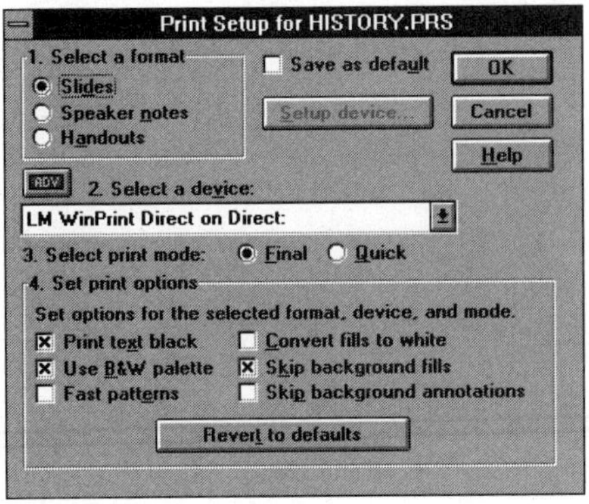


## Using Print setup

1. Choose Print setup from the File menu.
2. Select the item that you want to set up: Slides, Speaker notes, or Handouts.
3. Select the device you want to use for printing the selected item from the Select a device drop-down list.

   You do not have to choose the same device for Slides, Speaker notes, and Handouts.
4. Select the print mode: Final for the best possible looking stuff or Quick for those of you who are less patient.
5. Select the print options you want:
   - **Print text black:** Prints all text black and does not print drop shadows or sweeps.
   - **Use B&W palette:** Choose this option to print a color presentation on a black-and-white printer.

   Don't select B&W palette if you are already using a black-and-white palette, such as MONO.PL.

   - **Fast patterns:** Scales hatch and pattern fills to allow faster printing.
   - **Convert fills to white:** Changes solid, pattern, gradient, and bitmap fills to white.
   - **Skip background fills:** Select this option to ignore background fills when they are sent to a printer.
   - **Skip background annotations:** Select this option to ignore background annotations when they are sent to a printer.

6. If you change your mind after setting any of these options, click the Revert to defaults button to return all settings to their initial settings.
7. Click OK to close the Print Setup dialog box and return to the program.

TIP

To save these settings as new defaults, select the Save as default check box.

## Quick Presentations

Harvard Graphics contains seven professionally designed presentations: brainstorming session, business plan to partners, company profile, marketing plan, new product proposal, quarterly review, and training seminar.

If you want to follow the general direction of one of these presentations, open it and substitute your data and information for the material in the presentation.

### Using Quick Presentations

1. Choose Quick Presentations from the File menu to open the Quick Presentations dialog box.

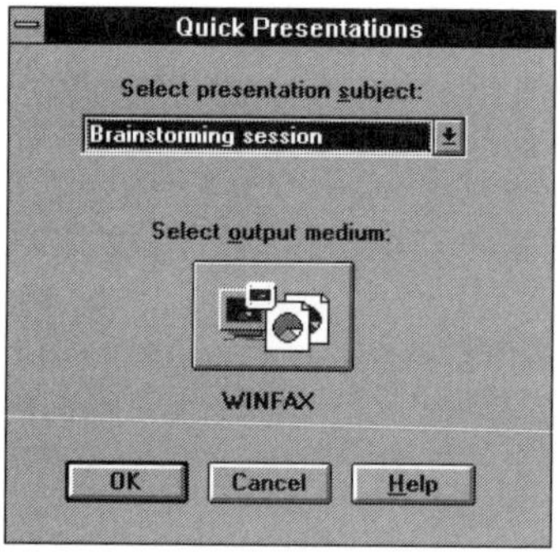


2. Select the presentation that you want to view or change from the Select presentation subject drop-down list.
3. Click the Select output medium button to open the Advisor.

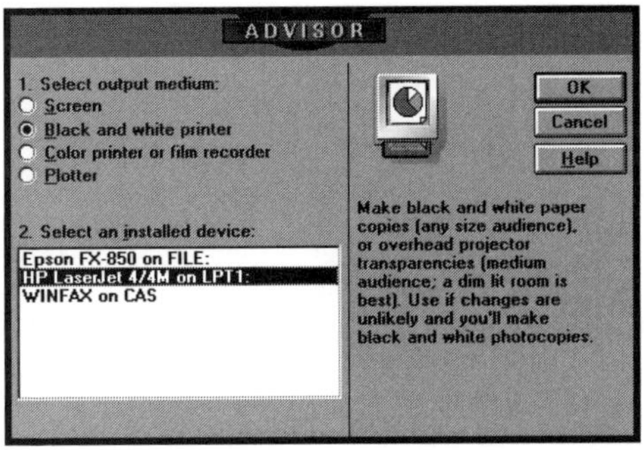


4. Select an output medium:
   - **Screen:** Use this option if you are going to change the presentation. The Quick Presentation appears on-screen.
   - **Black and white printer:** If you select this radio button, all black-and-white printers installed on your system will be listed. Select the one you want to use from the Select an installed device list.
   - **Color printer or film recorder:** If you select this radio button, color printers installed on your system are listed. Select the one you want to use from the Select an installed device list.
   - **Plotter:** Lets you choose from a list of any plotters installed on your system.
5. Click OK to close the Advisor and click OK again to open the quick presentation.

## More stuff

If you want to add a presentation of your own design to the list of quick presentations, save it in the HGW\PRES\QUICKPRS directory. The first 25 characters of the description you give the file in the Save As dialog box appear as one of the subjects in the Quick Presentations dialog box.

# Redo

If you are ever faced with the problem of wanting to undo what you undid, Redo is for you. Redo reverses the last undo that you did. Got it?

## Ribbon bar icon

## Digital rodent replacement

Ctrl + R

## Using Redo

Choose Redo from the Edit menu.

## More stuff

TIP

You can use Redo to reverse the last four Undo commands.

The Redo command is not available if you have

- not used the Undo command.
- saved the presentation (or if Autosave has saved it for you).
- switched to another view.
- opened the Data Form.
- displayed another slide.

# Rotate

Rotates a graphic.

## Using Rotate

1. Select the graphic that you want to rotate.
2. Choose Rotate from the Graphics menu. The cursor changes to a circular arrow, and the object grows a rotation handle.
3. Drag the handle to rotate the object.

## More stuff

You don't have to be awfully near the object when you drag the rotation handle.

# Ruler / Grid

Turns on or off the display of rulers and grids and sets the number of marks per inch.

## Using Ruler / Grid

1. Choose Ruler / Grid from the Options menu to open the Ruler / Grid Options dialog box.

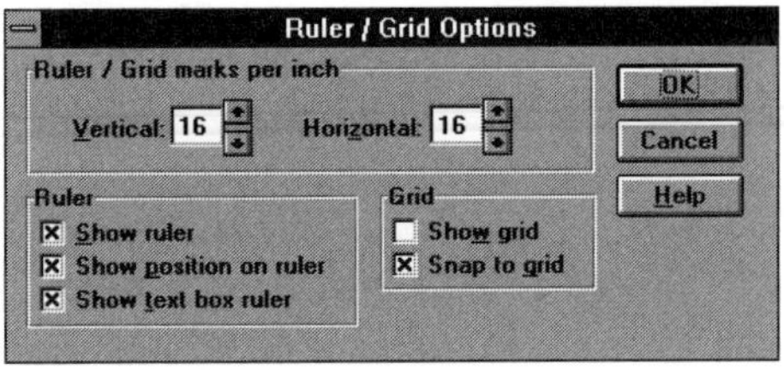


2. Set the number of marks per inch that you want to show on the ruler and grid in the Vertical and Horizontal boxes.
3. The check boxes in the Ruler area of the dialog box control the appearance of the ruler:
   - **Show ruler:** Check this box to display the ruler.
   - **Show position on ruler:** Check this box to have guidelines appear on the horizontal and vertical rulers at the position of the cursor.
   - **Show text box ruler:** Check this box to have a little ruler appear whenever you drag a text box into existence.
4. The check boxes in the Grid area of the dialog box control the appearance and behavior of the grid:
   - **Show grid:** Check this box to have the grid appear on the slide as a series of dots.
   - **Snap to grid:** Check this box to make the grid act like a magnet and attract anything that you drag near it. Useful for lining up stuff.
5. Click OK to close the dialog box and put the changes into effect.

# Save, Save As . . .

Saves a presentation to disk. When you save a presentation for the first time, the Save As dialog box opens to let you give it a name. Any subsequent save uses the same name, and the dialog box does not open. You also can use the Save As command to save an existing file in a different location or format under a different name.

## Ribbon bar icon

## Digital rodent replacement

Ctrl + S

## Using Save and Save as

1. Choose Save (or Save as) from the File menu.
2. If you selected Save and the drawing already has a name, the drawing is saved to disk.
3. If this is the first time the drawing has been saved, or if you selected Save as, the Save As dialog box opens.

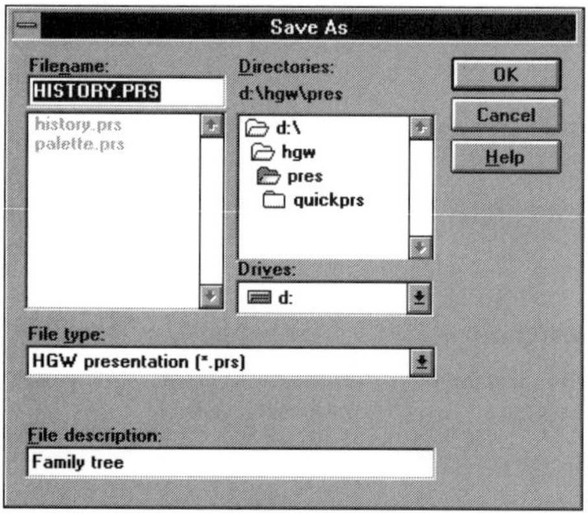


4. Give the file a name and select the drive and directory where it is to be stored.

5. If you want to save your presentation as a style, select HGW presentation style (*.STY or *.PRS) from the File type drop-down list.

   See Save Presentation Style for a discussion of styles.

6. Type a description of the file in the File description area. This description will help you find the presentation later.

7. Click OK.

## Save Presentation Style

A presentation style is made up of the master template, individual templates (slide and custom), background images, and color palettes. Saving the style enables you to use the same look for a series of presentations.

### Using Save presentation style

1. Choose Save presentation style from the Style menu to open the Save Presentation Style dialog box.

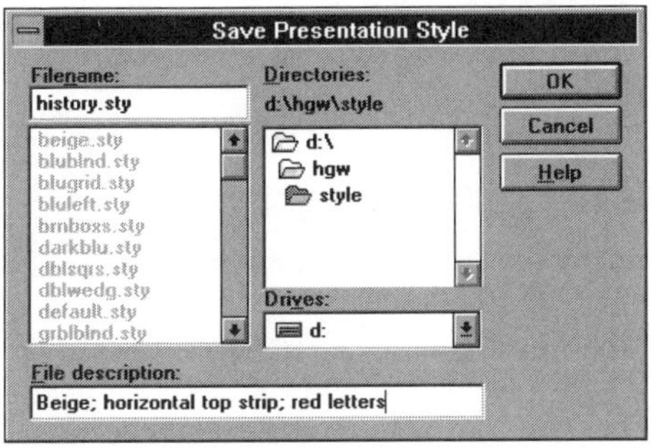


2. Give the style a name and select the drive and directory where it is to be stored.

   You should keep all your styles in the same directory because they are much easier to find when you do. The default directory for styles is HGW\STYLE.

3. Type a description of the style in the File description area. This description will help remind you of the style later.

4. Click OK to save the style and close the dialog box.

### More stuff

Be careful not to accidentally overwrite one of the styles that shipped with Harvard Graphics. If you do, and you want to use the erased style again, you have to reinstall the style from the Install disks.

## ScreenShow from Beginning

Runs your screen show starting at slide #1.

### Ribbon bar icon

### Digital rodent replacement

Ctrl + F2

### Using ScreenShow from beginning

To view the screen show, choose ScreenShow from beginning from the View menu.

## ScreenShow from Current Slide

Runs your screen show starting at the current slide.

### Ribbon bar icon

### Digital rodent replacement

Alt + F2

### Using ScreenShow from current slide

To view the screen show, choose ScreenShow from current slide from the View menu.

## Select All

Selects all objects in the work area.

### Digital rodent replacement

Ctrl + A

### Using Select all

Choose Select all from the Edit menu.

The objects that are selected when you choose this command depend on which view you use it from:

- **Outliner view:** Select all selects every line in the outline, visible or not.
- **Slide Sorter:** Select all selects every slide in the Sorter, visible or not.
- **Slide Editor:** Select all selects every object on the current slide.
- **Data Form:** Select all selects every cell that contains data (every line for text charts).

### More stuff

TIP

This command can be useful when you want to move every item on a slide but maintain the relative position of the items. After the items are selected, dragging one element repositions all of them.

You can use Select all to copy all the slides in a presentation (in Slide Sorter view) or all the items from one slide (in Slide Editor view) to another presentation.

## Select Presentation Style

Applies a new style to your presentation.

TIP

A presentation style consists of the master template, individual templates (slide and custom), background images, and color palettes. Styles allow you to maintain a consistent look for a series of presentations.

## Using Select presentation style

1. Choose Select presentation style from the Style menu to open the Select Presentation Style dialog box.
2. Select a style from the Filename drop-down list. The File description area indicates some of the characteristics of the style, and a representation of the style appears in the Slide template area. Select different slide styles from the Slide template drop-down list to see how they will appear.

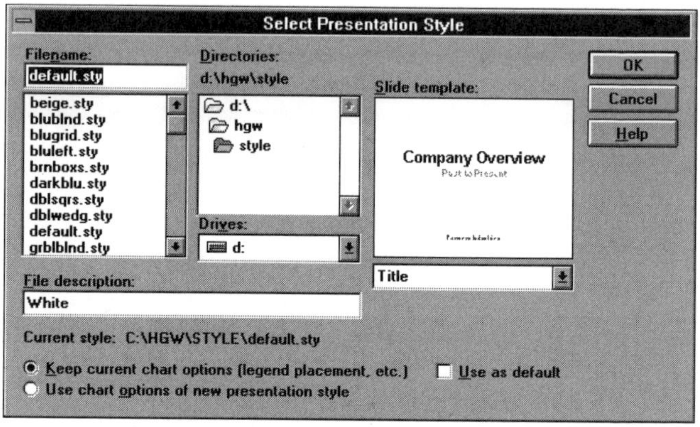


3. If you want to keep the current options (text placement, series, legend, frame, grid, and axis) but change the colors, click the Keep current chart options radio button. If you want to use the style's chart options, click the Use chart options of new presentation style radio button.
4. If you like this style so much that you want to use it most of the time, click the Use as default check box.

## More stuff

See Save Presentation Style to learn how to enter comments in the File description area.

# Send Mail

Sometimes you just want to gab a bit and send an e-mail message without leaving Harvard Graphics. Also, there are times when you simply have to get your work from one place to another, and regular mail just won't do. If you have an electronic-mail application that supports the MAPI or VIM interface standard (this is techno gobbledy-gook for "Can you e-mail in Windows?"), you can connect to, or put your work on, the electronic superhighway. Even from a car stuck in a traffic jam.

## Using Send mail

1. If you want to send a presentation, make it active and be sure that it is saved.
2. Choose Send mail from the File menu to open the Send Mail dialog box.

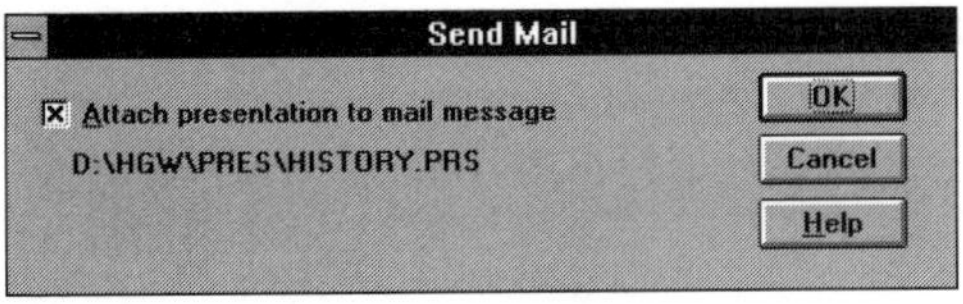


3. To attach the current presentation to the message, check the Attach presentation to mail message check box.
4. Click OK to transfer the presentation to your e-mail software.

## More stuff

TIP: If you are e-mailing a presentation to another location, make sure that all files linked to the presentation (animations, sounds, movies, and so on) are sent, too. If the files don't go with the presentation, they can't be played.

WARNING! Files, especially presentations with linked sound or movies, can grow to be horribly large. If you are going to e-mail a presentation over a modem connection, remember that it can take quite a while to send and receive, and be sure that it will fit on the recipient's computer.

# Series

Shows, hides, or changes the attributes of a series. A *series* is a set of related values that is represented in a chart by a pie, column, bar, line, and so on.

## Using Series

1. Make the chart active in the Slide Editor.
2. Choose Series from the Chart menu to open the XY Chart Series Options dialog box.
3. Select the series that you want to change in the Series list.
4. To display the selected series, check the Show series check box. To hide the selected series, deselect the Show series check box.
5. To display the selected series in the data table, check the Include series in data table check box. To hide the data, deselect the check box.

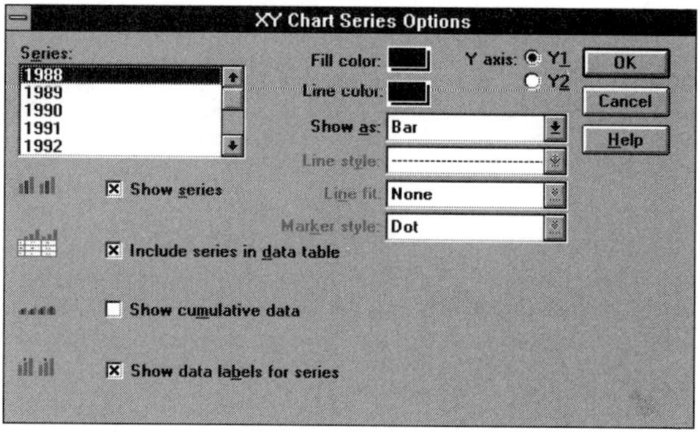


6. Choose Show cumulative data to show the series as a running total.
7. Select the Show data labels for series check box to include the label for the selected series.
8. Select the Fill and Line colors you want by clicking the appropriate box to open the color palette.
9. The Show as drop-down list lets you choose to display the selected series as a line, curve, area, or as points.
10. If the series is represented by a line, you can choose a line style from the Line style drop-down list.
11. If the series is represented by a line or points, you can choose a line fit from the Line fit drop-down list.
12. If the series is represented by a line, a curve, or points, you can choose a line marker from the Marker style drop-down list.

13. The Y-axis buttons assign the selected series to either the Y1 or Y2 axis.

# Series Statistics

Displays all sorts of mysterious statistical information about a selected series.

## Using Series statistics

1. Make a chart active in the Slide Editor or Outliner.
2. Choose Series statistics from the Chart menu to open the Series Statistics dialog box.

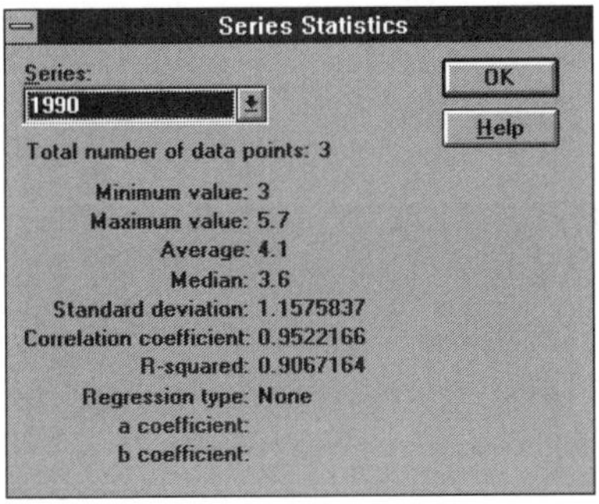


3. Select the series you want to explore from the Series drop-down list.

## More stuff

Use this command to impress your friends and neighbors.

# Set Anchor Point

Use this command to glue a text box to a selected location. After it's activated, the anchor point in the text block remains fixed. Any text added to the box grows from that point.

## Using Set anchor point

1. Create a text box in a slide.
2. Choose Set anchor point from the Text menu to open the Anchor Point dialog box.

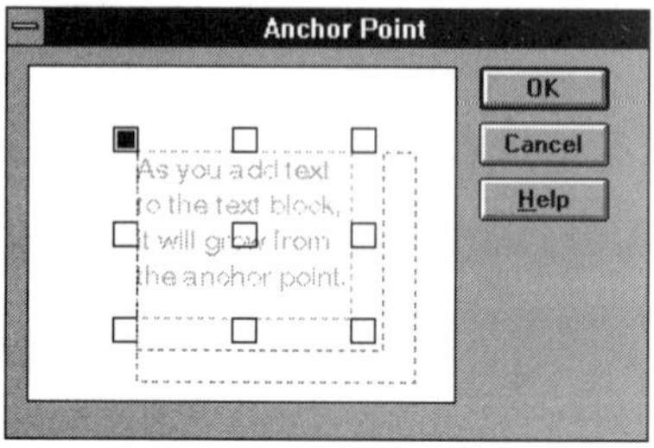


3. Click the box that you want to serve as the anchor.
4. Click OK.

# Set Bullet Attributes

Controls the look of bullets.

## Using Set bullet attributes

1. Select a text box or bullet list.
2. Choose Set bullet attributes from the Text menu to open the Bullet Attributes dialog box.

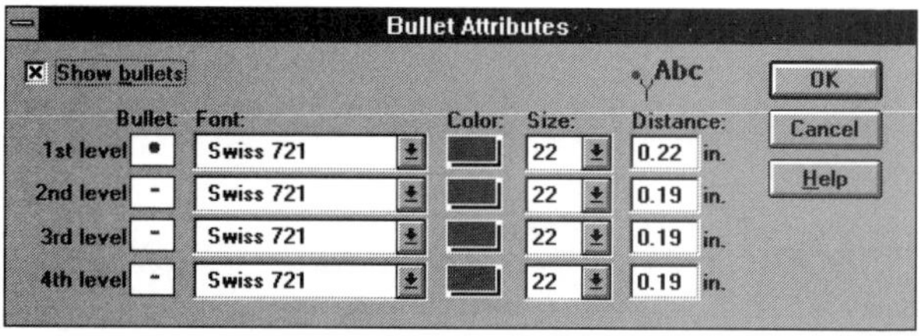


3. Use the Show bullets check box to toggle the display of bullets on or off.
4. Select the attributes that you want for each level of bullet by clicking the Bullet, Font, Color, Size, and Distance (from text) boxes.

## More stuff

You can have up to nine levels of bullets, but attributes that you set for the fourth level apply to all subsequent bullets (levels 5, 6, 7, 8, and 9).

# Show Subtitle & Footnote

This command is found in the Outline menu. When active, it shows subtitles and footnotes in the presentation outline.

See Outline for more information about this command.

# Slide Editor

Allows you to view an individual slide.

## Toolbar icon

## Using Slide Editor

Choose Slide Editor from the View menu.

# Slide Sorter

Allows you to view all slides in the current presentation.

## Toolbar icon

## Using Slide Sorter

1. Choose Slide Sorter from the View menu to open the Slide Sorter view.

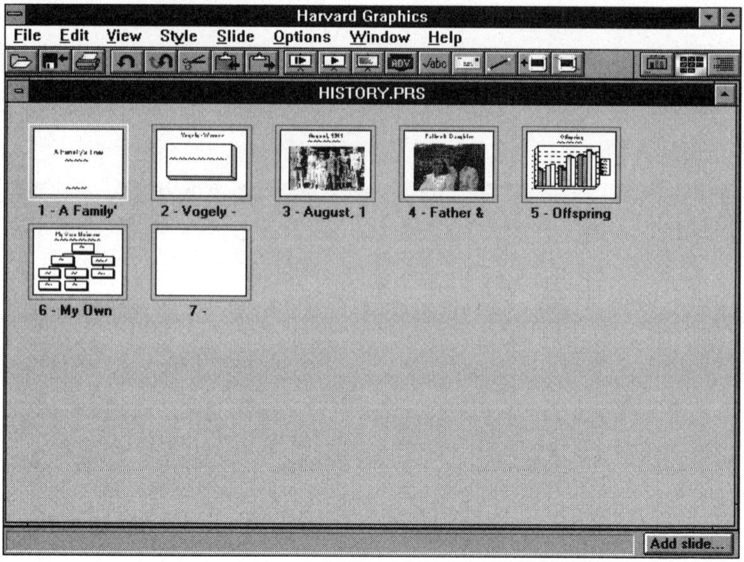


2. To rearrange the order of the slides, click the slide you want to move and then drag it to a new position.
3. You also can use Slide Sorter view to delete slides, copy and paste slides between different presentations, add sound, import and export slides, or link slides as OLE objects.

See Add Sound, Import, Export, or the other individual commands for more information about using them in Slide Editor or Slide Sorter views.

## Slide Templates

Harvard Graphics comes with a wide variety of predefined styles. Each type of chart within a style has a template that defines its colors, text positions, and so on. You can edit, apply, or create new templates by using the Slide templates command.

See Select Presentation Style for information about using styles.

### Using Slide templates

1. Choose Slide templates from the Style menu in either Slide Editor or Slide Sorter view to open the Slide Templates dialog box.

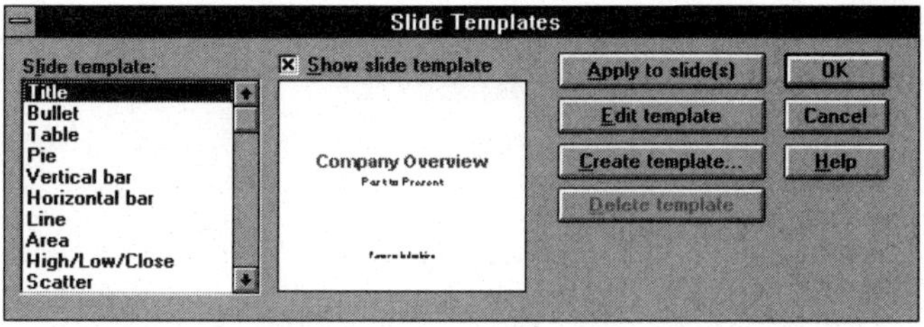


2. Select the template that you want to use, modify, or create from the Slide template scroll list.
3. Click the Show slide template check box to see what the template looks like.
4. To change parts of the template, click the Edit template button. This action opens the template with the selected slide showing. Make any changes that you want and then click the Back to slide button, which is located at the bottom-right corner of the screen.

To make a new template:

1. Click the Create template button to open the Create Slide Template dialog box.
2. Give your creation a name.

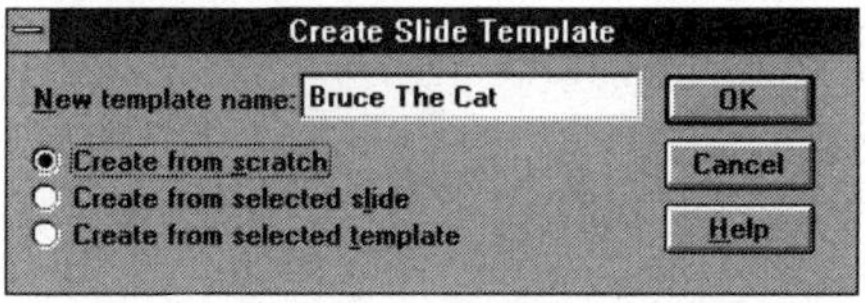


3. Choose where you want to start: creating from scratch, using the selected slide as a base, or using the current template.
4. Click OK to open the template with the selected slide showing. Make any changes that you want and then click the Back to slide button, which is located at the bottom-right corner of the screen.
5. The Delete template button is now active; if you hate what you did, you can blow it away.

# Special Effects

Lets you add a drop shadow, frame, or sweep to the selected object, text, bitmap, or symbol.

## Using Special effects

1. Select the object, text, bitmap, or symbol that you want to gussy up.
2. Choose Special effects from the Graphics menu to open the Special Effects dialog box.

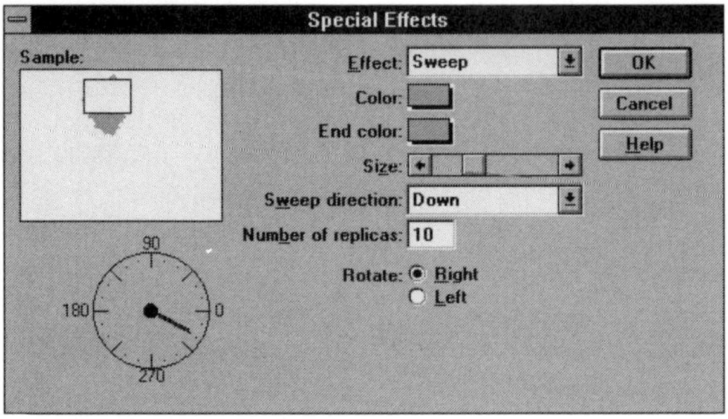


3. Choose the Effect you want:
   - **None:** Applies no special effect or removes whatever is there.
   - **Frame:** Changes the attributes of the frame (color, transparency, and size).
   - **Drop shadow:** Gives the impression of depth.
   - **Sweep:** Applies rotation and the appearance of movement to the frame.
4. If appropriate for the effect, choose from the following:
   - **Frame:** Choose color by clicking the color box to open the palette and selecting Transparency, Size, 3-D frame, and Fit frame to text.
   - **Drop shadow:** Choose color by clicking the color box to open the palette and selecting Transparency.

- **Sweep:** Choose starting and ending colors by clicking the color boxes to open the palette and select Size, Sweep direction, Number of replicas, and direction and angle of rotation.

5. Click OK to apply the effect.

## More stuff

Refer to the Sample viewing area to see the effects of your choices.

If you really think that this stuff is keen, flip to the F/X section.

# Symbol Library

Harvard Graphics comes with a whole truckload of symbols. Stick 'em in a presentation to give it some character or to relieve the stress caused by your message.

## Ribbon bar icon

## Using Symbol Library

1. Choose Symbol Library from the Graphics menu to open the Open Symbol File dialog box.
2. Select the group of symbols that is closest to the one you want. Descriptions of the collections appear in the File description area.

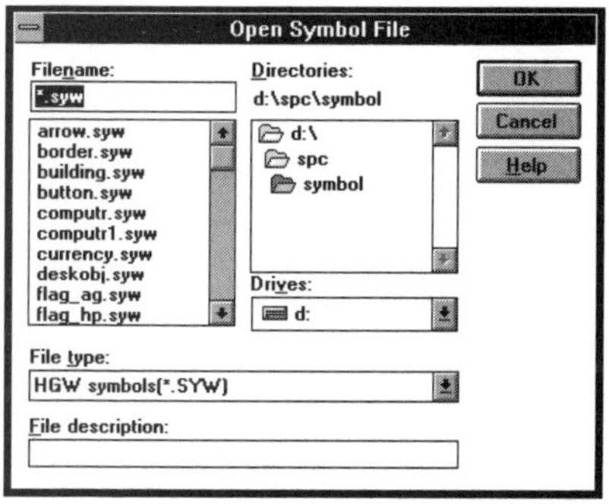

3. Click OK to open the Symbol Library Manager with your selection displayed.

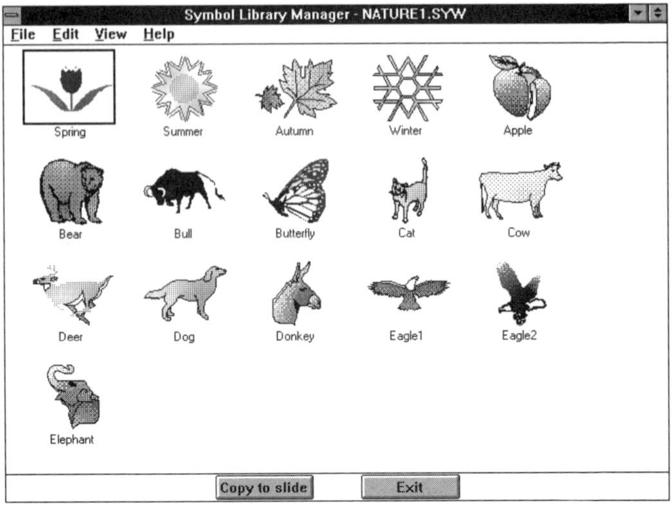


4. Select the symbol that you want and click the Copy to slide button.
5. Click Exit to close the Symbol Library Manager and return to your slide with the symbol displayed.
6. Move or resize the symbol as you want.

# Tile

Harvard Graphics allows you to have several presentations open at the same time. To avoid being sent to bed without your supper because of slovenly screen habits, you may want to have all your pictures neatly tiled, one right next to the other. The Tile command does this automatically, saving you much frustration and sidelong glances from your peers.

## Digital rodent replacement

Shift + F4

## Using Tile

If you have a deep-seated need to be neat or a disapproving significant other, choose Tile from the Windows menu to display all your open presentations, tidily ordered.

# Undo

Reverses the actions (up to four) that you have performed. The Undo command name changes as you perform actions.

## Digital rodent replacement

Ctrl + Z

## Using Undo

Choose Undo from the Edit menu.

## More stuff

The Undo command is not available if you have

- saved the presentation (or if Autosave has saved it for you).
- switched to another view.
- checked spelling.
- opened the Data Form.
- displayed another slide.

# Ungroup

Tears asunder groups that have been put together with the Group command.

## Digital rodent replacement

Ctrl + U

## Using Ungroup

1. Select the group that you want to ungroup.
2. Choose Ungroup from the Graphics menu.

## More stuff

TIP

You can often use Ungroup on imported graphics, like WMF files and symbols, to change them or to delete unwanted areas and objects from them.

# Unindent

This command is found in the Outline menu. When selected, it unindents the position in an organization chart one level.

## Digital rodent replacement

Shift + Tab

REFERENCE

See Outline for more information about this command.

# Zoom

## Zoom in

## Zoom out

## Actual size

## Fit in window

Lets you get a good look at what you're doing.

## Using Zoom

Choose Zoom from the View menu to open the Zoom flyout menu. Then choose one of these options:

- **Zoom in:** Magnifies the screen and gives you a close-up view of a portion of your drawing. Zoom in magnifies a selected object. You can zoom in up to four times.
- **Zoom out:** Zooms out by a factor of two each time you select the command.
- **Actual size:** Displays the slide at the same size that it will print or appear in a ScreenShow.
- **Fit in window:** Zooms to bring all objects in the slide into view.

# The Part of Tools

The part of tools gives a brief explanation of the nine major tools that you can use in Harvard Graphics.

## Selection Tool

Use the selection tool to select an object for moving, resizing, copying, deleting, grouping, and other similar stuff. (You have used the selection tool if little square handles appear around the object.)

## Text Tool

You use the text tool to add new text by drawing a text box (click the tool and then drag to create a box where you want it) or to edit selected text (click the tool and then click the text box that you want to edit).

## Line Tool

Use the line tool to draw straight lines. If you want to constrain the line to be vertical, horizontal, or some multiple of 45 degrees, hold down the Shift key as you draw.

You can change line characteristics by using the Line Attributes command.

## Polyline Tool

The polyline tool comes in two flavors: one for drawing open, straight-lined shapes of two or more points, and the other to draw curved shapes of three or more points. To access the polycurves tool, point to the polylines tool, press the mouse button for a second or two, and then drag over to its icon.

If you want to constrain the line or curve to be vertical, horizontal, or some multiple of 45 degrees, hold down the Shift key as you draw.

To finish drawing a polyline or polycurve, either release the mouse button and press the Esc key or click the right mouse button.

## Freehand Tool

Use this tool to draw irregular lines and curves. If you end a shape near where you started it, Harvard Graphics automatically closes the shape and applies the current fill and outline attributes.

## Rectangle Tool

Use this tool to draw square-cornered or round-cornered rectangles. To access the rounded tool, point to the rectangle tool, press the mouse button for a second or so, and then drag over to the rounded tool.

To constrain the shape to a perfect square, hold down the Shift key while you drag the rectangle into place.

## Oval Tool

Use this tool to draw ovals. To constrain the shape to a perfect circle, hold down the Shift key while you drag the shape into place.

# Polygon Tool

The polygon tool comes in two flavors: one for drawing closed straight-lined shapes and the other to draw curved ones. To access the rounded polygon tool, point to the polygon tool, press the mouse button for a second or two, and then drag over to its icon.

If you want to constrain the line or curve to be vertical, horizontal, or some multiple of 45 degrees, hold down the Shift key as you draw.

To finish drawing a polygon, release the mouse button and press the Esc key or click the right mouse button.

# Eyedropper Tool

You use the eyedropper tool to copy the attributes of a selected object and then apply them to another object. Attributes include fill, line weight, color, text size, and font. The tools are located under the eyedropper tool. To access them, point to the eyedropper tool, press the mouse button for a second or two, and then drag over to the icon that you want.

The copy attributes tool has the up-pointing arrow. Use it to click the object that you want to copy. The paste attributes tool has the down-pointing arrow. After you copy attributes, use this tool to click another object and assign the copied attributes to it.

# Part II

# Harvard F/X

Harvard F/X is cool! One of the keener things about F/X is that you can use it as a stand-alone program to do wild stuff with text and copy it to other Windows programs.

Do something real gnarly and copy F/X to the Windows Clipboard and then paste it into another Windows program, such as Word for Windows, Write, or Paintbrush.

# Align

Aligns the selection handles on two or more objects.

## Digital rodent replacement

Ctrl + I

## Align dialog box

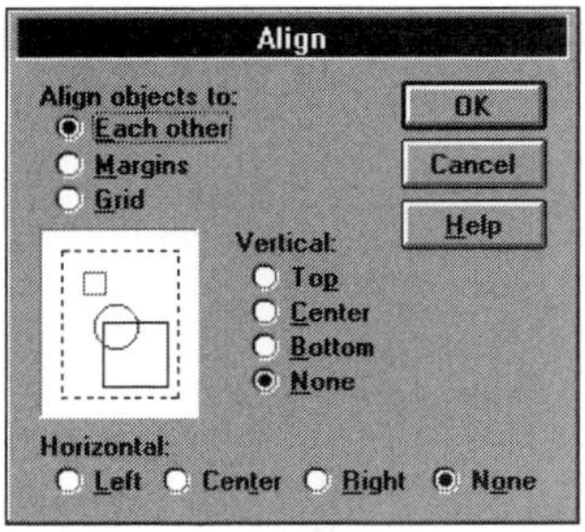


## Using Align

To line up two or more objects:

1. Select the objects by Shift+clicking each in turn.
2. Choose Align from the Arrange menu to open the Align dialog box.
3. Choose whether you want to align the objects to Each other, the Margins of the page, or the Grid.
4. Choose one box from the Vertical area (Top, Center, Bottom, or None) and one from the Horizontal area (Left, Center, Right, or None).
5. Click OK.

## More stuff

TIP

The alignment pretty much follows the selection handles around each object. For example, if you have a text object selected and its box is larger than the text it contains, the alignment affects the entire box. This could leave the text looking like it was not properly positioned. To fix this problem, resize the text box to conform to the length of the text.

# All Attributes (Line and Fill)

This handy command enables you to change all the line and fill attributes in one place. You can obtain the same results by using the individual commands: Fill; Line; Line style, and Line width.

## Digital rodent replacement

Ctrl + E

## Using All attributes

To change the attributes of existing lines and fills:

1. Select the object with the selection tool.
2. Choose All attributes from the Color menu to open the Line and Fill Attributes dialog box.

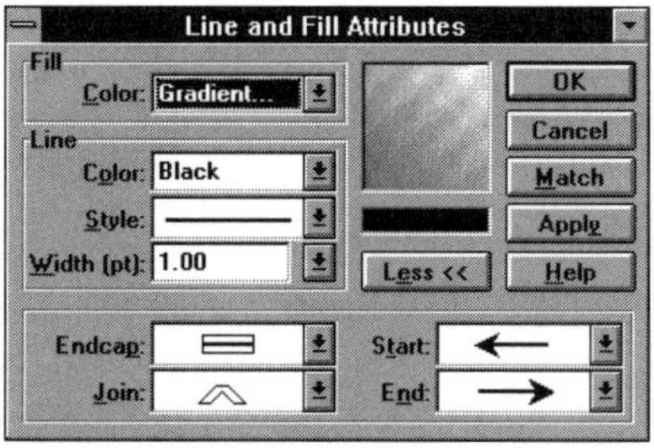


3. Select Fill attributes.

   Each attribute is covered under the Fill command.
4. Select Line attributes.

   These attributes are discussed under the Line, Line Style, and Line Width commands.
5. Clicking the More button opens an additional area of the dialog box that allows you to set Endcap styles, Join miters, and pointers on the ends of lines (Start and End drop-down lists). If your dialog box shows a Less button, you already have the "More" displayed. This goes to prove the old axiom, "Less is more."
6. Click Apply to make the changes to the selected object and then click OK to close the dialog box.

## More stuff

If you change the Line and Fill settings without an object selected, you modify the default settings.

To duplicate the attributes of an existing object, select the object and then click the Match button in the Line and Fill Attributes dialog box. The settings stay selected, and they then can be applied to another object.

See Match Attributes and Apply Attributes for an easier way to copy attributes from one object to another.

# All Attributes (Text)

Even though you can set some text attributes individually by using the Font, Size, and Style commands, using them can become quite a pain when you want to change more than one attribute at a time. The All attributes command opens a handy dialog box that lets you change these attributes at the same time, as well as set spacing, capitalization, and alignment.

## Digital rodent replacement

Ctrl + T

## Using All attributes (Text)

To change the attributes of existing text:

1. Select the text box with the selection tool.
2. Choose All attributes from the Text menu to open the Text Attributes dialog box.

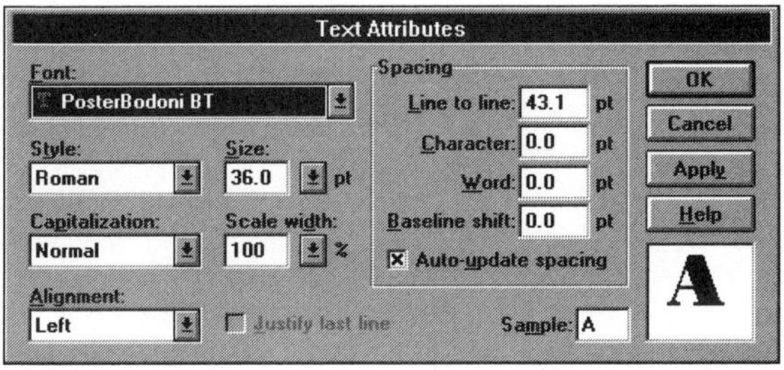

3. Choose the Font, Style, and Size you want from the drop-down lists or type the desired specifications in the boxes.

   For information about Font, Style, and Size, see the individual commands in this part.

4. Select the type of Capitalization you want from the drop-down list.

5. If you want to make the text fatter or thinner without changing its height, enter a new number in the Scale width box.

   You also can adjust the width (or height) of text by dragging the selection handles of the text box.

6. Select the Alignment you prefer. If you choose Justify from the drop-down list, you have the option of justifying the last line of text by clicking in the Justify last line check box.

7. The Spacing area allows you to modify the Line to line spacing and the space between individual Characters and Words, as well as shift the baseline of selected text up or down (use a negative sign to shift down) to get a superscript or subscript effect.

8. When all the options are set the way you want, click the Apply button.

9. Click OK to close the dialog box.

## More stuff

If you make any changes in the Text Attributes dialog box without first selecting any text, you change the defaults for any subsequent text boxes.

# Apply Attributes

A handy way to apply outline and fill attributes to objects. Works just about like All attributes (Color), but you can apply the line and fill without first having to select the object. This command is useful for duplicating one set of line and fill attributes to several different objects.

## Digital rodent replacement

Ctrl + Y

## Using Apply attributes

1. With no object selected, choose All attributes from the Color menu to open the Line and Fill Attributes dialog box.

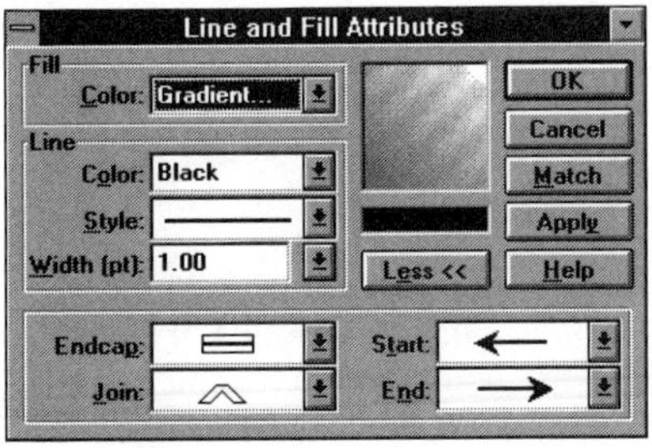


2. Select Fill attributes.

   Each attribute is covered under the Fill command.

3. Select Line attributes.

   These attributes are discussed under the Line, Line Style, and Line Width commands.

4. Clicking the More button opens an additional area of the dialog box that allows you to set Endcap styles, Join miters, and pointers on the ends of lines (Start and End drop-down lists).

5. Click Apply to make the changes to the selected object and then click OK to close the dialog box. This action sets the default line and fill attributes.

6. Select the object to which you want to apply these attributes and then choose Apply attributes from the Color menu.

## More stuff

You can apply these attributes to as many objects as you want by selecting the object and pressing Ctrl+Y or by invoking Apply attributes from the Color menu.

# Blend Two Paths

The objective of a blend is to take a starting object and transform it into an ending one, all the while doing some fancy stuff along the way. In this respect, blending is kinda like morphing for the economically distressed. You can change one thing into another, and you don't even need to buy a ton of multimedia stuff. All the intermediate steps are left on-screen to view, however, so it isn't exactly the same. That's why it's called *blending,* I guess.

## Using Blend two paths

All blends start with a beginning object and an ending one, so to construct a blend, follow these steps:

1. Draw your beginning and ending objects and separate them with enough space to let F/X do its thing. This procedure is pretty much a trial-and-error one. The objects have to be far apart if you are using bunches of intermediate steps but less so if you are using only a few intermediate steps.
2. Select both objects by Shift-clicking each one.
3. Choose Blend two paths from the Effects menu to open the Blend Two Paths dialog box.

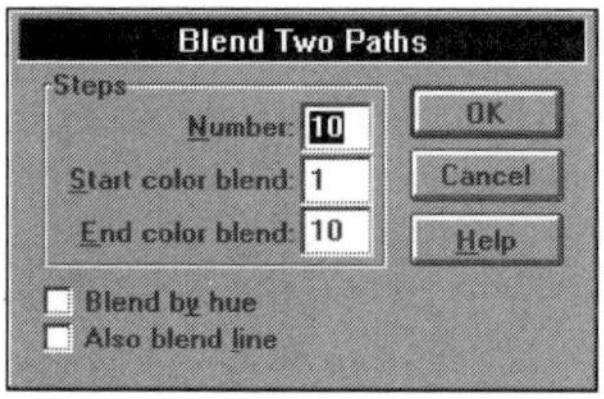


4. Fill in the number of intermediate shapes you want between the beginning and ending objects in the Number box.
5. Fill in the step number where you want to start blending the colors of the two objects in the Start color blend box. This number is almost always 1.
6. Fill in the step number where you want to end blending the colors of the two objects in the End color blend box. This number is almost always the same as the one you entered in the Number box.
7. Select the Blend by hue check box to create a rainbow effect (using more colors).
8. Select Also blend line to include the line attributes in the blend.
9. Click OK.

### More stuff

When you are blending two objects, the one on top is the object that is at the front of the painting order. In other words, if you want one object to be on top, select it and choose the Move to front command from the Arrange menu (Ctrl+F is the shortcut).

## Break Apart

Sometimes things just don't work out. The best-laid combinations fall short of expectations. Choose Break apart to uncombine objects that have been stuck together with the Combine command.

### Using Break apart

To break combined objects apart:

1. Select the combined object.
2. Choose Break apart from the Arrange menu.

## Cascade

F/X allows you to have several images open at the same time. As wonderful as this feature is, it creates the likelihood that these images will be scattered willy-nilly about your work area. To avoid being chastised by the less slovenly, use the Cascade command to neatly stack your stuff in inspection order.

### Digital rodent replacement

Shift + F5

### Using Cascade

If you have a deep-seated need to be neat, choose Cascade from the Windows menu to display all your open images, tidily stacked.

# Circular Copy

This pretty neat command copies a selected object over and over while rotating it at the same time.

## Using Circular copy

1. Select the object that you want to rotate.
2. Choose Circular copy from the Effects menu to open the Circular Copy dialog box.

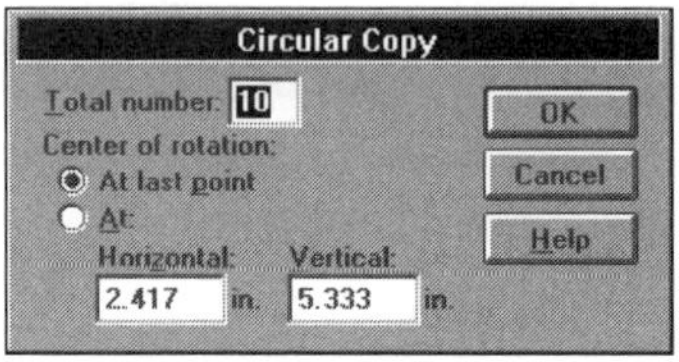


3. Fill in the Total number of times you want the object copied, including the original.
4. Select the center of rotation. Choose At last point to rotate the object around the last point, or enter a distance in the Horizontal and Vertical boxes to offset the rotation from the center point.

# Clear

Removes the currently selected object from the picture.

## Digital rodent replacement

Del

## Using Clear

1. Select the object that you want to remove.
2. Choose Clear from the Edit menu.

## Combine

Combines the selected objects into a single object.

### Using Combine

1. Select the objects that you want to combine.
2. Choose Combine from the Arrange menu.

### More stuff

The most totally awesome and way-cool thing to do with Combine (to me, anyway) is using it to create a *clipping hole* (a hole cut in one shape that allows you to see what's behind it). It's really simple to do. Here's an example: Draw a box and then place some text (use a fat font) inside it. Select the text and then choose Convert to paths from the Text menu. Combine the box and converted text and then fill the resulting object with a color or a fountain fill. Where the text is becomes transparent, and stuff behind the object shows through. Cool.

The same thing happens when you combine two objects such as circles and squares. The area in which the objects overlap becomes transparent, creating a clipping hole.

## Convert to Paths

Converts a selected text object to a series of curves. After an object has been converted to curves, you can move its individual nodes about with the select points tool.

### Using Convert to paths

To convert a text object to paths:

1. Select the object that you want to convert.
2. Choose Convert to paths from the Text menu.

### More stuff

TIP

If you convert text objects with overlapping characters to curves, the places where the characters overlap become transparent.

After an object has been converted to curves, you cannot change it back again (unless you use the Undo command). Also, after you convert text to a curve, it is no longer a character (unless its name is Fried Freddie) and it cannot be edited with the text tool — or spell-checked, for that matter.

# Copy

Copying an object makes a duplicate of it and places the duplicate on the Windows Clipboard.

## Ribbon bar icon

## Digital rodent replacement

Ctrl + C

## Using Copy

1. Select the object to copy.
2. Choose Copy from the Edit menu.

## More stuff

After you copy an object to the Clipboard, you can paste it into most Windows applications simply by choosing Paste from the application's Edit menu.

# Create Pattern

REFERENCE

This command is, frankly, bunches of fun. You can create a custom fill to use in any object you want. For example, use the technique discussed in the Combine command to create an object with a clipping hole (you can even use your logo). Make this new creation a fill and save it to use later.

## Using Create Pattern

1. Draw or select an object that you want to use as a pattern fill.
2. Choose Create pattern from the Color menu.

## More stuff

When you create a pattern, it becomes the current fill and can be applied to any object you want.

TIP: To keep a pattern for later use, save your drawing in the \HFX\PATTERN directory. You then can access it from the Fill flyout menu of the Color menu.

# Cut

Cutting an object removes the selected stuff and places it on the Windows Clipboard.

## Ribbon bar icon

## Digital rodent replacement

Ctrl + X

## Using Cut

1. Select the object to cut.
2. Choose Cut from the Edit menu.

## More stuff

After you cut an object to the Clipboard, you can paste it into most Windows applications simply by choosing Paste from the application's Edit menu.

# Display

Changes the items displayed on-screen.

## Using Display

1. Choose Display from the Options menu to open the Display dialog box.

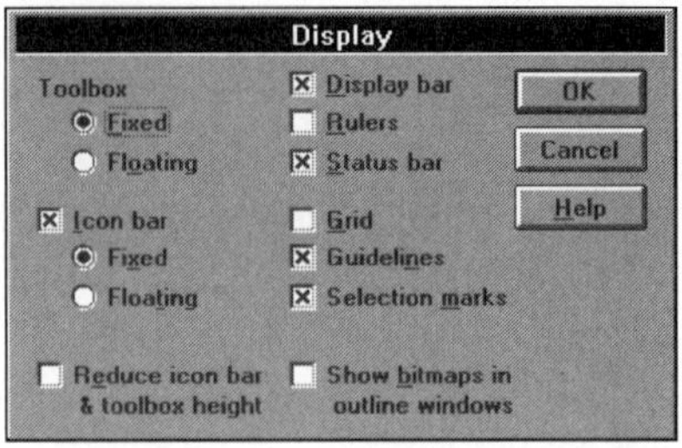


2. Select the display options you prefer:

   - **Toolbox:**

     **Fixed:** Select this option if you want the toolbox to remain glued to the left side of the screen.

     **Floating:** Selecting this option lets you move the toolbox about to get it out of the way. You also can resize it to make its shape more convenient.

   - **Icon bar:**

     **Fixed:** Select this option if you want the icon bar to remain glued to the top of the screen.

     **Floating:** Select this option to move the icon bar about to get it out of the way. You also can resize it to make its shape more convenient.

   - **Display bar:** Toggles the display bar on and off.
   - **Rulers:** Shows or hides rulers.
   - **Status bar:** Shows or hides status information in the title bar (the information appears in the title bar, strange and wonderful, for sure).
   - **Grid:** Displays or hides a grid of nonprinting lines to use as an aid. The grid is set up by choosing Measurements from the Options menu.
   - **Guidelines:** Displays or hides guidelines to use as an alignment aid. You set up guidelines by choosing Guidelines from the Options menu.
   - **Selection marks:** Shows or hides selection handles.
   - **Reduce icon bar & toolbox height:** Makes the bars smaller.
   - **Show bitmaps in outline windows:** Shows or hides bitmaps when you're viewing in Outline mode.

# Duplicate

Creates a copy of the selected object(s).

## Digital rodent replacement

Ctrl + D

## Using Duplicate

1. Select the object that you want to duplicate.
2. Choose Duplicate from the Edit menu.

## More stuff

If you duplicate by pressing Ctrl+D or by choosing the Duplicate command from the Edit menu, the copy of the object is placed a little above and to the right of the original. You can change this offset by moving the duplicate to a new position. This distance then becomes the default.

TIP

You can nudge a selected object about with any arrow key.

# Exit

Quits F/X and returns you to wherever you started the program (to either the Windows Program Manager or the File Manager).

## Digital rodent replacement

Alt + F4

## More stuff

When you choose the Exit command from the File menu and have drawings open that have not been saved, a message dialog box appears and asks whether you want to save your work. To save the stuff, choose Yes. The drawing is saved if it has a name, and the Save As dialog box appears if the drawing has not been saved before. To abandon the changes, choose No.

# Export . . .

Saves your drawing and text in a format that can be read or used by another program.

## Using Export

1. Choose Export from the File menu to open the Export dialog box.

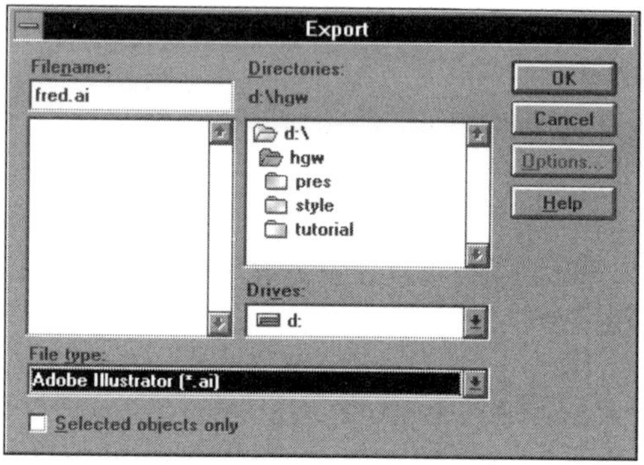


2. Give the file a name and select the type from the File type drop-down list.
3. If you want to export only selected parts of a drawing, click the Selected only check box, and only those parts that you selected in the original are exported.
4. Click OK, and another dialog box may open, depending on the type of graphic format you are using.
5. Enter any necessary information or accept the defaults (your best bet unless you really know what you are doing).
6. Click OK.

## More stuff

If you are exporting to a program that uses a PostScript printer, use the EPS format. If you are not exporting to print as a PostScript file, it is a good idea to use the following formats:

| *If You Are Exporting to:* | *Use This Format:* |
|---|---|
| Adobe Illustrator | AI |
| Ami Professional | WMF |
| Arts & Letters | WMF, EPS (using Decipher) |
| Macintosh-based vector programs | AI |
| Micrografx Designer | CGM |
| PageMaker | WMF |
| PC Paintbrush | PCX |
| Word for Windows | WMF |
| WordPerfect | WPG |

# Extrude

Extrudes are cool, boss, far out, and gnarly. An *extrude* takes a two-dimensional object and makes it look three dimensional by adding surfaces to it. Think of a pasta machine: the extrusion is the flour mixture oozing out of the die.

## Using Extrude

1. Select the object that you want to extrude.
2. Choose Extrude from the Effects menu to open the Extrude dialog box.

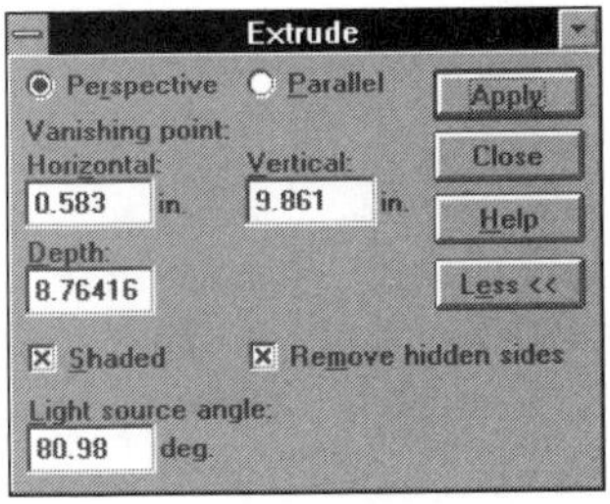


3. To make your extrude look like it disappears off into the distance, click the Perspective radio button. To make it not disappear into the distance, click the Parallel radio button.

4. If you choose Perspective, you can set the vanishing point by entering numbers in the Horizontal, Vertical, and Depth boxes. However, it is a lot easier to drag the little X-shaped doodad that is placed on-screen when you choose the Perspective option. Play with it a bit and you'll see what I mean.
5. If you choose Parallel, you can set the angle and depth of the extrude.

   TIP: To see more options, click the More button. (If you see Less, you already have More.)
6. If you want to add shadows and depth to the extrusion, select the Shaded check box. Doing so places a neat little smiling sun on-screen that represents the source of light. You can drag the little sun-thing to change the angle that the light shines on the object, or you can put an angle measurement in the Light source angle box.
7. Click Apply.
8. Drag stuff around until you have it the way you want it. When all is okay, click Close.

TIP: Extrudes take bunches of computer power. If you are using a memory-challenged computer, you may want to find something else to do while your computer wrestles with the calculations.

# Fill

Selects fill attributes.

## Using Fill

1. Choose Fill from the Color menu. The flyout menu contains the following options:

   TIP: The number of colors that you see are limited by the capabilities of your computer and monitor. You will be able to see anywhere between 16 and 16 million different colors.

   - **None:** Makes objects transparent.
   - **Black and White:** Apply a fill of the selected color.
   - **Mix:** Opens the Mix Fill Colors dialog box. Click the color you want in the palette or color wheel, or enter values in the tint and color boxes. The Model drop-down list lets you select from the four standard color-mixing models. If you aren't sure which one you want

and you need to send your work out to be placed on film or separated for printing, ask the folks at your service bureau which one they want you to use. If your stuff is going to stay in-house or just be displayed on computers, don't worry about it.

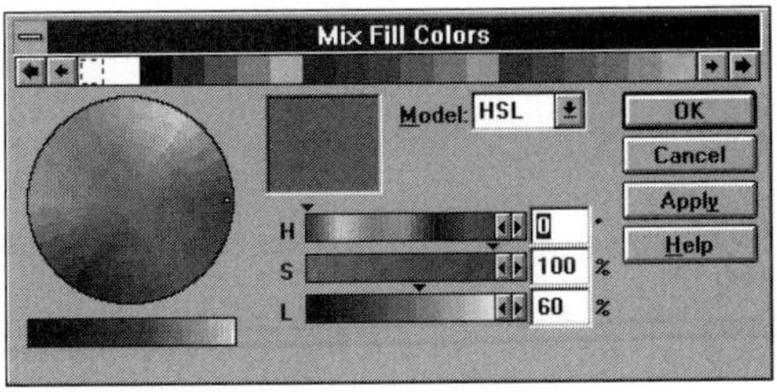


- **Named:** Opens the Named Colors dialog box. Click the color you want or enter its name in the Color name area.

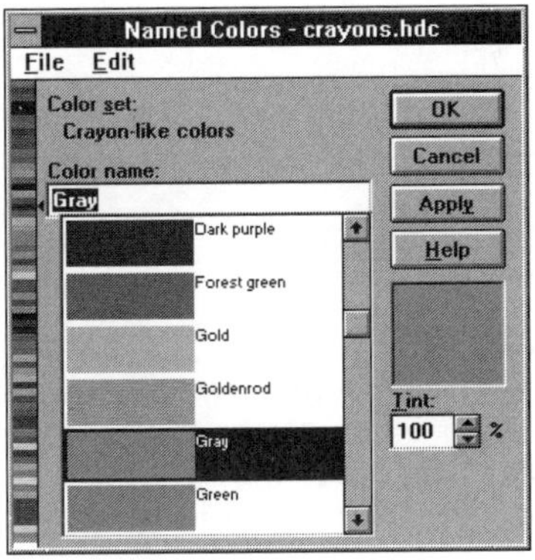


- **Gradient:** Opens the Gradient Fill dialog box. Select the starting and ending colors (Color 1 and Color 2) and drag the pointer in the preview area to change the angle of the gradient. If you choose a Stepped fill, you get the opportunity to select the number of bands it will take to go from one color to the other.

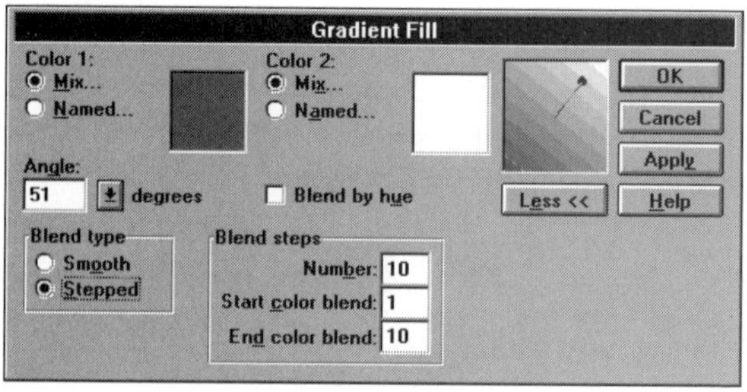


- **Radial:** Opens the Radial Fill dialog box. Select the Edge and Center colors and the shape that the fill is to assume. You can drag the center of the fill, represented by a circle, to get offset effects.

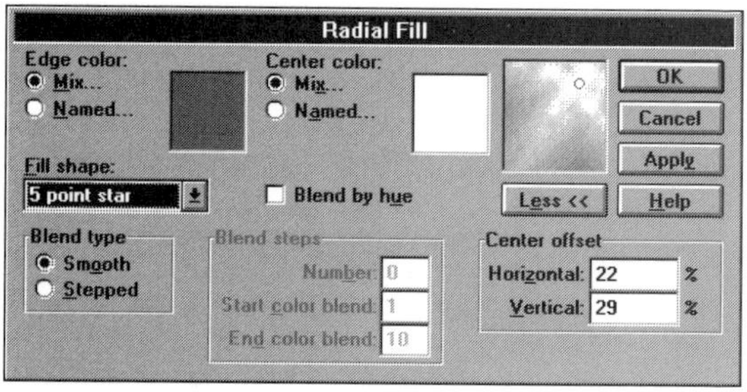


- **Pattern:** Opens the Pattern Fill dialog box. You can choose the size of the fill tiles and their offset from the grid or page. Click the Library button to open another dialog box that enables you to choose from the patterns supplied with F/X or from those you have created.

See Create Patterns to learn how to roll your own.

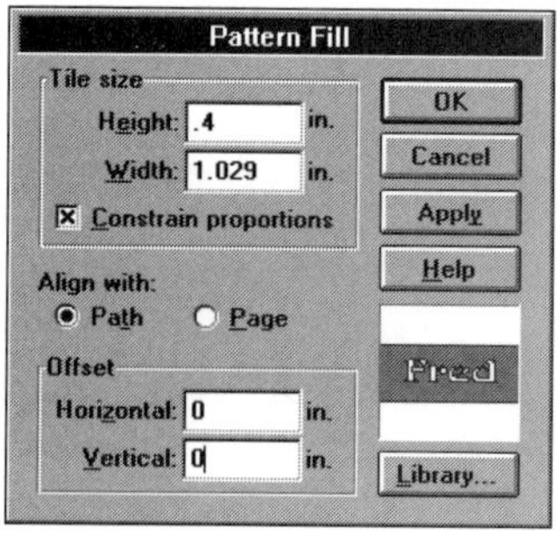

- **Textured:** Opens the Textured Fill dialog box. Select the colors you want and then choose a style from the Style drop-down list.

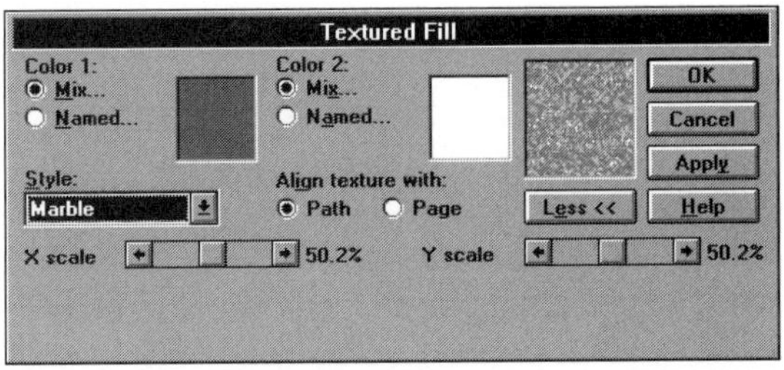


## Font

Selects the font to use for text.

### Using Font

1. Choosing Font from the Text menu opens a list of the most recently used fonts. If the one you want is shown, click it to select it.
2. If the font you want is not listed, click Other to open the Select Font dialog box.

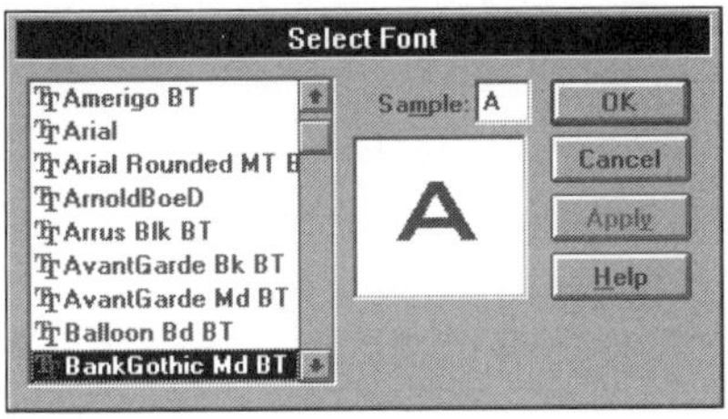


3. Select the font you want to use from the scroll list.
4. Click OK.

### More stuff

See All Attributes (Text) for a way to change more font stuff than just the typeface at once.

# Full Screen Preview

Displays a full-screen view of your drawing. Press any key to return to normal view.

## Digital rodent replacement

F2

## Using Full screen preview

1. Choose Full screen preview from the Window menu.
2. Press any key to exit.

## More stuff

You cannot edit in full-screen preview.

# Group

Makes all selected objects into a group and allows them to be selected and modified as a single object.

## Ribbon bar icon

## Digital rodent replacement

Ctrl + G

## Using Group

1. Select the objects that you want to group (Shift+click).
2. Choose Group from the Arrange menu.

## More stuff

Using groups makes it easy to change attributes.

## Guidelines

If you choose to display the rulers in the Display dialog box (Options⇨Display), you normally just drag guidelines into the desktop from one of the rulers by placing the cursor anywhere on the ruler and dragging a guideline into the work area. Sometimes you may demand greater precision, and the Guidelines command then becomes useful.

### Using Guidelines

Guidelines take their measurements from the 0,0 point of the rulers, or the *origin.* You can adjust the zero point by dragging the crosshair icon from the box where the horizontal and vertical rulers meet to the location where you want the new zero points to be placed.

1. Choose Guidelines from the Options menu to open the Guidelines dialog box. You also can open this dialog box by double-clicking a ruler.

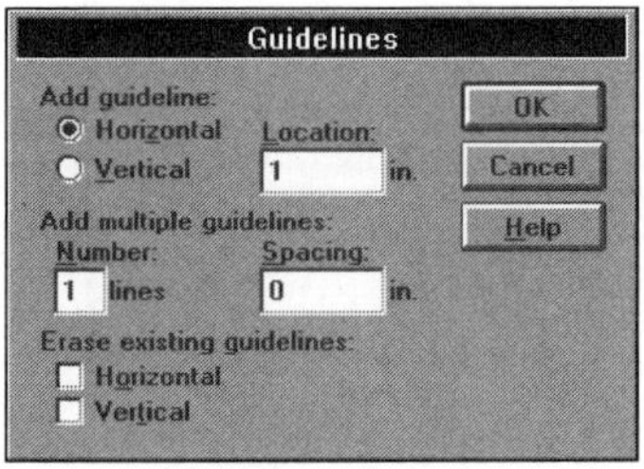


2. To add a single guideline, select either the Horizontal or Vertical guideline radio button and enter the measurement in the Location area for the guide you want to add.
3. To add a series of guidelines, select either the Horizontal or Vertical guideline radio button and enter the measurement in the Location area for the first line. Then enter the number of lines you want in the Number box and the amount of space between them in the Spacing box.

If you want the guidelines to be "sticky" and attract objects, choose Snap to grid & guides from the Options menu.

# HGW Symbol Library

Harvard Graphics comes with a whole truckload of symbols. You can use them as a part of an F/X creation, too.

## Ribbon bar icon

## Using Symbol Library

1. Choose HGW Symbol Library from the File menu to open the Open Symbol File dialog box.

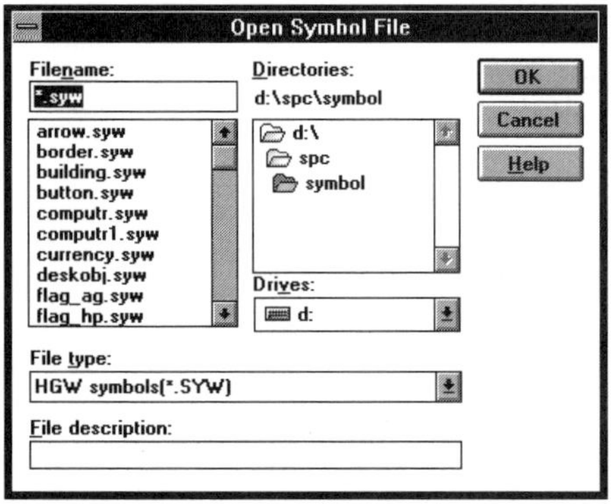


2. Select the group of symbols that is closest to the one you want. Descriptions of the collections appear in the File description block.
3. Click OK to open the Symbol Library Manager with your selection displayed.

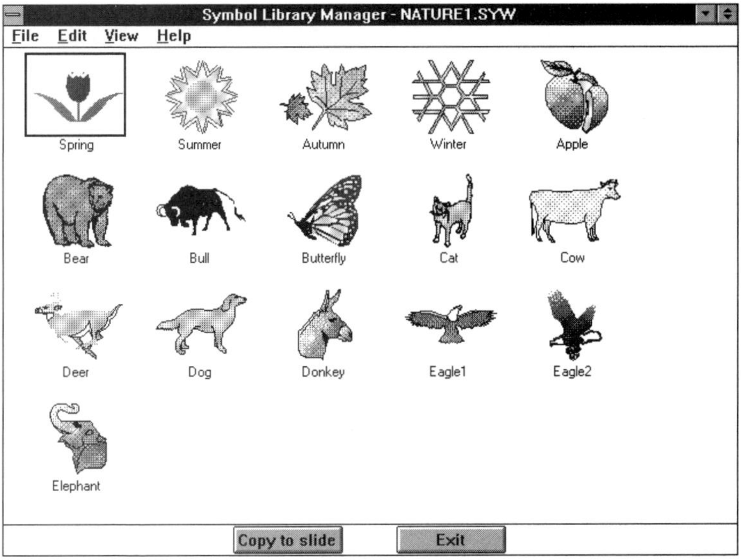


4. Select the symbol you want and click the Copy to slide button.
5. Click Exit to close the Symbol Library Manager and return to your slide with the symbol now displayed.
6. Move or resize the symbol as you want.

# Import

Brings in drawings created in other programs or merges other F/X graphics into the current drawing.

## Ribbon bar icon

## Using Import

1. Choose Import from the File menu to open the Import dialog box.

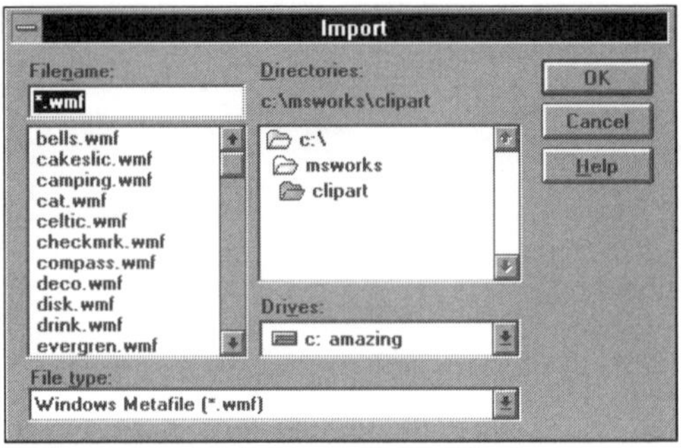


2. Select the type of file from the File type drop-down list. You often can get by with the *.* selection.
3. Navigate through the drives and directories to find the file you want to import.
4. Click OK.

TIP: If you aren't getting quite the results you want, you may want to try using the following file extensions to import your stuff.

| *If You Are Importing from:* | *Use This Format:* |
|---|---|
| Adobe Illustrator | AI (EPS) |
| Arts & Letters | AI (EPS), Clipboard |
| CorelDRAW | CDR, Clipboard |
| CorelTRACE | CorelTRACE EPS |
| Harvard Graphics | CGM |
| Lotus 1-2-3 | Lotus CGM (more recent versions) or Lotus PIC |
| Lotus Freelance Plus | CGM |
| Macintosh-based vector programs | AI |
| Micrografx Designer, Graph Plus | AI (EPS) |
| Scan Gallery | TIF |
| WordPerfect | WPG |

## Line

Changes the color attributes of lines.

## Using Line

Choose Line from the Color menu. The flyout menu contains the following options:

TIP

The number of colors that you see is limited by the capabilities of your computer and monitor. You will be able to see anywhere between 16 and 16 million different colors.

- **None:** Hides the outline.
- **Black and White:** Apply a fill of the selected color.
- **Mix:** Opens the Mix Line Colors dialog box. Click the color you want in the palette or color wheel or enter values in the tint and color boxes. The Model drop-down list lets you select from the four standard color-mixing models. If you aren't sure which one you want and you need to send your work out to be placed on film or separated for printing, ask your friendly service bureau personnel which one they want you to use. If your stuff is going to stay in-house or just be displayed on computers, don't worry about it.

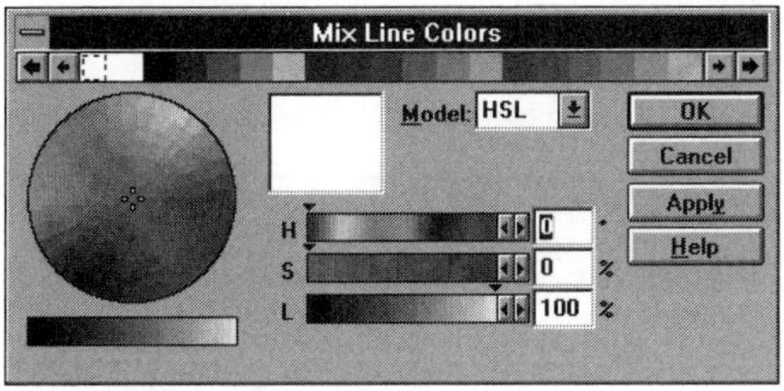


- **Named:** Opens the Named Colors dialog box. Click the color you want or enter its name in the Color Name area.

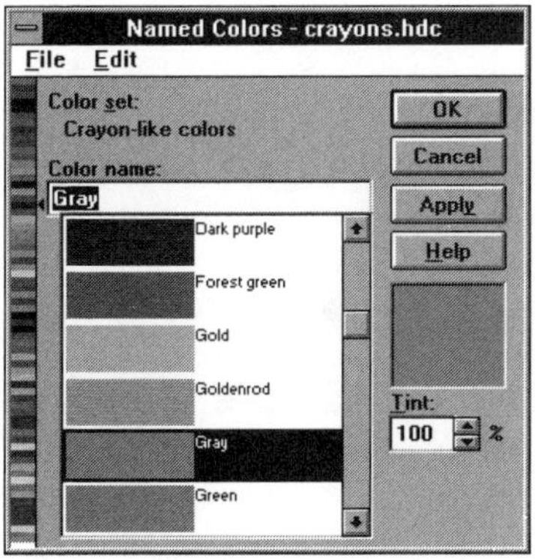

- **Textured:** Opens the Textured Line dialog box. You can choose the line color and one of the preset textures from the Style drop-down list. A representation of the line appears in the preview area.

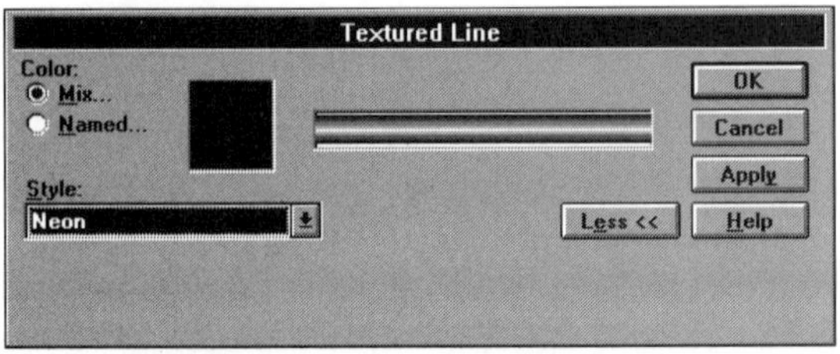


TIP

Use this command with a line selected to change that line only. Use it with no line selected to change the default.

## Line Style

Choose different line types.

### Using Line style

1. Choose Line style from the Color menu.
2. If a line that you want to use appears in the flyout menu, click it to make it active.
3. If you prefer to build your own line, select Other to open the Line Style dialog box. In this dialog box, you can define up to four different "pieces" of your custom line by stipulating each segment's length and the space between it and the next segment.

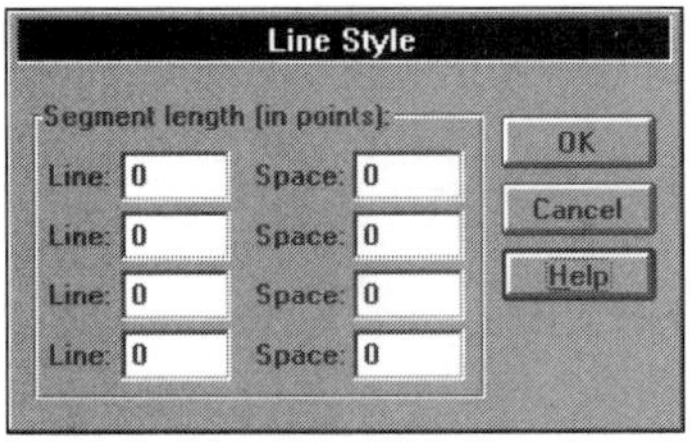

### More stuff

TIP

Use this command with a line selected to change that line only. Use it with no line selected to change the default.

## Line Width

Changes the width of lines.

### Using Line width

1. Choose Line width from the Color menu.
2. If a width that you want to use appears in the flyout menu, click it to make it active.
3. If you prefer to build your own line, choose Other to open the Line Width dialog box and type in the desired width in points.

### More stuff

TIP

Use this command with a line selected to change that line only. Use it with no line selected to change the default.

## Linear Copy

This pretty neat command copies a selected object over and over in a line.

### Using Linear copy

1. Select the object that you want to rotate.
2. Choose Linear copy from the Effects menu to open the Linear Copy dialog box.

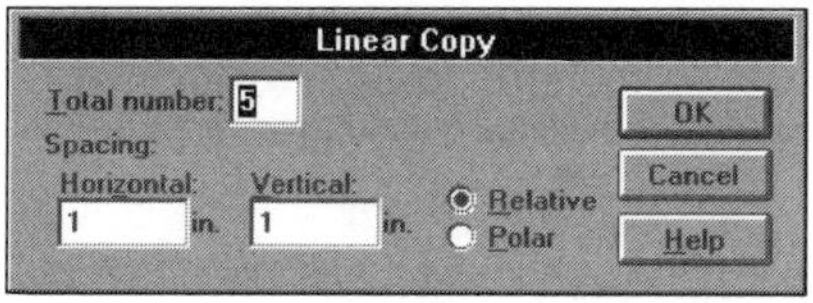

3. Fill in the Total number of times you want the object copied, including the original.
4. Choose either Relative (actual distance) or Polar (combination of distance and degree of slope).
5. Click OK.

# Lock

Use this command to nail an object into place so that it cannot be selected without being unlocked first.

## Digital rodent replacement

Ctrl + L

## Using Lock

1. Select the object(s) that you want to lock.
2. Choose Lock from the Arrange menu.

## More stuff

If you want to unlock the objects, choose Unlock from the Arrange menu.

# Match Attributes

A handy way to copy outline and fill attributes from objects. Used with Apply attributes, this command is useful for duplicating one set of line and fill attributes to several different objects.

## Digital rodent replacement

Ctrl + M

## Using Match attributes

1. Select the object whose outline and fill colors you want to copy.

2. Choose Match attributes from the Color menu. Doing so changes the current line and fill settings to those of the selected object.
3. Select the object(s) to which you want to apply these attributes and then choose Apply attributes from the Color menu.

## More stuff

You can apply these attributes to as many objects as you want by selecting the object and pressing Ctrl+Y or by invoking Apply attributes from the Color menu.

# Measurements

Changes the unit of measure, how much an object will be nudged when you press an arrow key, the angle used when constraining lines with the Shift key, and the distance between gridlines.

## Using Measurements

1. Choose Measurements from the Options menu to open the Measurements dialog box.

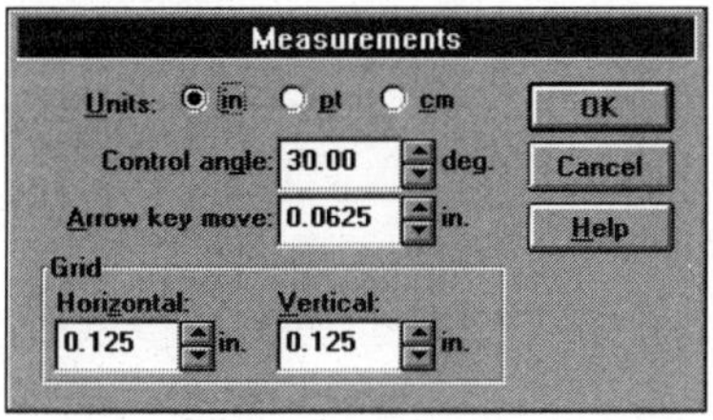


2. Modify the settings you want:
   - **Units:** Change the measurement on the rulers and many dialog boxes to inches, points, or centimeters.
   - **Control angle:** Sets the angle to which lines are constrained when the Shift key is pressed.
   - **Arrow key move:** Sets the distance that a selected object is nudged when an arrow key is pressed.
   - **Grid:** Establishes the Horizontal and Vertical separation of gridlines.
3. Click OK.

# Move

## To front

## To back

## Forward by one

## Backward by one

Rearranges the stacking order of objects in a drawing.

### Digital rodent replacements

To front: Ctrl + F

To back: Ctrl + B

Forward by one: Shift + F

Backward by one: Shift + B

### Using Move

1. Select the object or objects that you want to reposition.
2. Choose Move from the Arrange menu.
3. Select the movement that you want from the flyout menu.

# New

Clears the current drawing so that you can create a new one.

### Digital rodent replacement

Ctrl + N

### Using New

Choose New from the File menu.

### More stuff

If the current drawing has not been saved, a prompt appears, giving you the opportunity to save the current drawing.

TIP

The new drawing uses the same settings that were in effect for the old one (Page Setup, Object Fill, Outline, and so on).

## New Outline

F/X allows you to have up to six windows open at the same time. These windows are either outline windows or preview windows. Outline windows draw faster than preview windows, but preview windows show more detail.

### Using New outline

To open a new outline window, choose New outline from the Window menu.

## New Preview

REFERENCE

See also New Outline.

### Using New preview

To open a new preview window, choose New preview from the Window menu.

## Next Window

Allows you to cycle through open windows.

### Digital rodent replacement

Ctrl + F6

## Using Next window

Choose Next window from the Window menu to make the next window on-screen active.

# Open

Loads a drawing into F/X.

## Ribbon bar icon

## Digital rodent replacement

Ctrl + O

## Using Open

1. Choose Open from the File menu to open the Open dialog box.

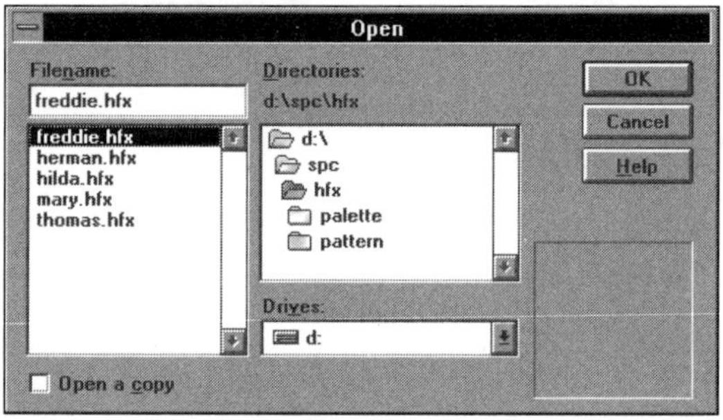


2. Enter the filename in the Filename box or use the Drives and Directories boxes to locate the drawing. A thumbnail representation of the drawing appears in the preview area.
3. If you want to open a copy of the drawing so that you don't mess up the original, click the Open a copy check box.
4. Click OK.

## More stuff

You can use wildcards in the Filename box. For example, entering **ex*.*** shows a list of all files beginning with *ex* in the selected directory.

# Page Setup

Changes page size, margins, orientation, and print options.

## Using Page setup

1. Choose Page setup from the File menu to open the Page Setup dialog box.

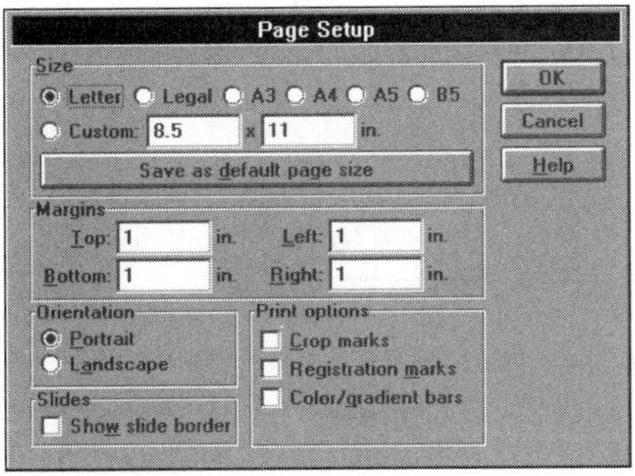


2. Select the options you want:
   - **Size:** Select the paper size that you want to use. If the size you want is not listed, select Custom and enter the measurements you want. If you will be using the same size page over and over, click the Save as default page size button.
   - **Margins:** Enter the Top, Bottom, Left, and Right margin measurements.
   - **Orientation:** Select Portrait (tall and thin) or Landscape (short and portly).
   - **Slides:** If you are printing to a film recorder, select the Show slide border check box to display a border around the slide. (You should select Landscape orientation, too.)

- **Print options:**

  **Crop marks:** Selecting this check box prints marks on the pages that indicate where the pages should be cut.

  **Registration marks:** Prints marks on pages, especially on color separations, that allow the pages to be exactly aligned.

  **Color/gradient bars:** Prints color tones on the pages that allow color matching.

# Palette

## Get

## Save

Because there are zillions of possible color combinations, it's helpful to narrow the choices somewhat. A *palette* is a selection of 150 or so colors that the software designers think go well together. It is represented by the row of color boxes that go along the top of the screen.

## Using Palette

To open a different selection of colors (F/X ships with 12 different choices, and you can define as many more as you want):

1. Choose Get from the Palette flyout menu on the Options menu. Doing so opens the Get Palette dialog box.

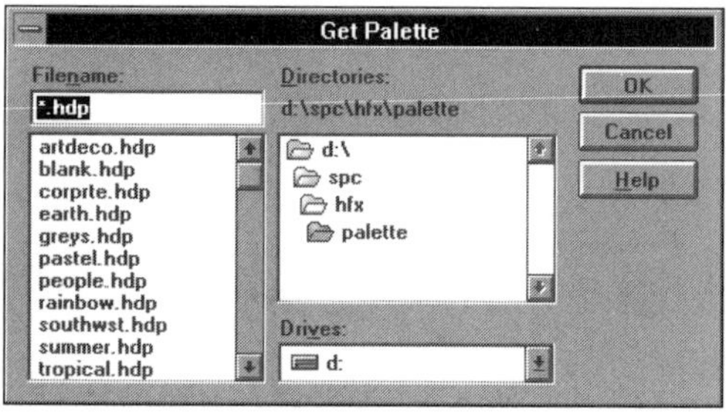


2. Choose the palette you want and click OK.

To change a palette:

1. Press Ctrl and click a color box in the existing palette. This action opens the Mix Colors dialog box.
2. Select or mix the color to which you want to change the square.
3. Click OK. The color of the selected square is now changed.
4. Choose Save from the Palette flyout menu on the Options menu. This action opens the Save Palette dialog box.

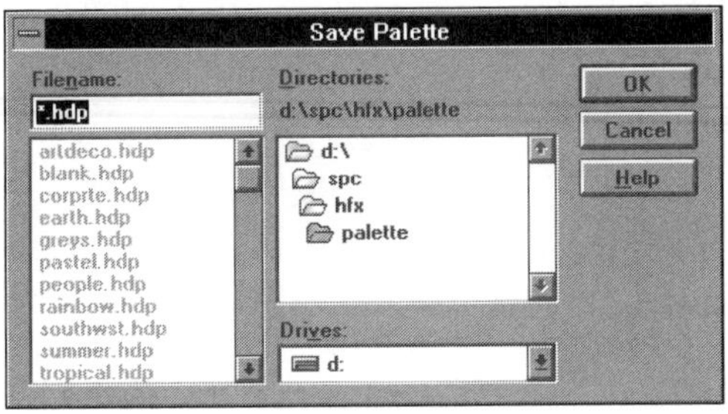


5. Give your new creation a name.
6. Click OK.

## More stuff

If you want to put an object's fill or outline color on the palette, select the object and then Ctrl+Shift+click the color square you want to replace.

# Paste

Pastes Clipboard contents into drawing.

## Ribbon bar icon

## Digital rodent replacement

Ctrl + V

## Using Paste

1. Be sure the object you want to paste into F/X is on the Clipboard.
2. Choose Paste from the Edit menu.

# Paste on Path

Plops the contents of the Clipboard onto each control point of a selected object.

## Using Paste on path

1. Cut or copy the object that you want to paste to the Clipboard.
2. Select the path that you to want to paste the object on.
3. Choose Paste on path from the Effects menu.

## More stuff

Control points are the ends of a line and the places where direction changes. You can use this command to highlight direction changes or to add repeated text to objects.

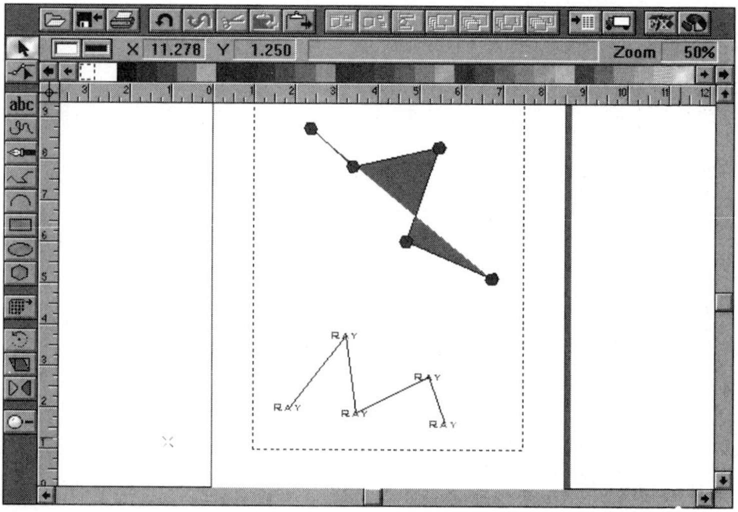

# Paste Special

Pastes Clipboard contents into a drawing and allows you to specify the format of the information.

## Using Paste special

1. Be sure that the information that you want to paste is on the Clipboard.
2. Choose Paste special from the Edit menu. This action opens the Paste Special dialog box.

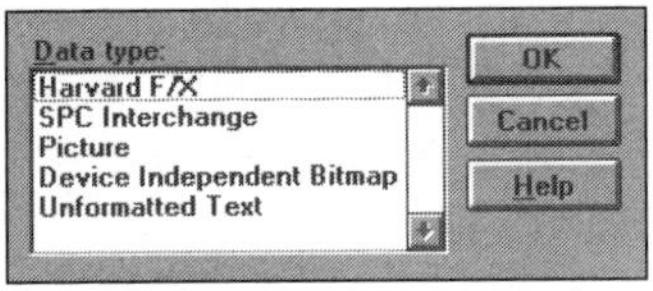


3. Select the Data type you want. Data type lets you choose which format you want to use. Several programs allow you to use different formats of information, such as RTF and ASCII. Choices include Picture (for WMF files), Bitmap (for DIB or DDB files), SPC Internal (for files created in Harvard Graphics or F/X), and Unformatted text.
4. Click OK.

# Path Effects

## Meld

## Intersect

## Subtract

## Punch

Changes how intersecting and overlapping paths act.

## Using Path effects

There are four different flavors of path effects.

**Meld** combines two or more objects into one:

1. Select the objects that you want to meld.
2. Choose Meld from the Path effects flyout menu in the Effects menu.

   - When objects are melded, they can be broken apart by using the Break apart command.
   - The melded object assumes the attributes of the object at the top of the painting order.
   - If the objects overlap, the outline of the intersecting parts is removed when the objects are melded.

**Intersect** creates a new object from the overlapping areas of two or more objects:

1. Select two or more overlapping objects.
2. Choose Intersect from the Path effects flyout menu in the Effects menu.
3. The common areas of the selected objects become a new object.

   The new object that results from the Intersect assumes the attributes of the object that was at the top of the painting order.

**Subtract** is pretty much the reverse of the Intersect command. Any overlapping areas are removed from the selected objects:

1. Select two or more overlapping objects.
2. Choose Subtract from the Path effects flyout menu in the Effects menu.
3. The portion of the lower object that is overlapped is removed.

   - The Subtract command removes the common area of the uppermost object from all other objects in the stack.
   - To see the effect, drag the subtracted object out of the way.
   - Use the Subtract command to cut holes in objects.

**Punch:** Pretty much like the Subtract command, except the new object is composed of the areas that are cut out of the images:

1. Select two or more overlapping objects.

2. Choose Punch from the Path effects flyout menu in the Effects menu.

   To see the effect, drag the overlapping object out of the way.

   If you punch three or more objects, the new object assumes the attributes of the object deepest in the stack.

# Perspective

## Add

## Remove

## Permanent

## Copy perspective

## Paste perspective

Lets you make a two-dimensional object look like it goes way back over there or comes at you off the page. (Think of a railroad track zipping off over the horizon, the rails getting closer as the track gets farther away.)

## Using Perspective

To add perspective to an object:

1. Select the object to which you want to apply perspective.
2. Choose Add from the Perspective flyout menu of the Effects menu. Doing so selects the select points tool and surrounds the object with handles.

   See Select Points Tool in the Part of Tools following this section.
3. Drag the handles in or out to mimic the perspective that you want.

To keep your perspective uniform throughout your work, see Copy Perspective in this section.

To remove perspective from an object:

1. Select the object.

2. Choose Remove from the Perspective flyout menu of the Effects menu.

To make a perspective permanent, so that you can import it into other applications:

1. Select the object.
2. Choose Permanent from the Perspective flyout menu of the Effects menu.

To copy perspective from one object to another:

1. Select the base object.
2. Choose Copy perspective from the Perspective flyout menu of the Effects menu.
3. Select the destination object.
4. Choose Paste perspective from the Perspective flyout menu of the Effects menu.

## More stuff

TIP

Choose Quick F/X from the Effects menu to apply a variety of prebuilt special effects.

# Preferences

Provides a way to change some of the defaults and speed up memory- or CPU-challenged computers.

## Using Preferences

1. Choose Preferences from the Options menu to open the Preferences dialog box.

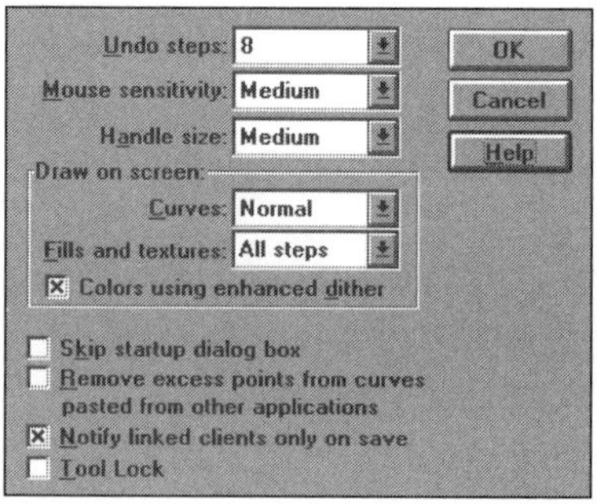

2. Change your preferences.

   - **Undo steps:** F/X remembers either the last 2, 4, 8, or 16 actions you performed. You can set this number here. The higher the number, the more work the computer has to do. Leave it at 16 unless you have tried everything else you can think of to make your machine run faster.
   - **Mouse sensitivity:** Sets how much you have to tickle the mouse to make it move. Choose Low, Medium, or High.
   - **Handle size:** If you are having problems clicking the mouse on selection handles, you can make the handles bigger. Select Small, Medium, or Large.
   - **Curves:** This option sets the way F/X draws curves on-screen. It does not affect printing. If your machine is running very slowly, you can speed the thing up by choosing Faster from this menu. If you have CPU and memory to waste, choose Smoother. Normal is for the rest of us.
   - **Fills and textures:** If your machine is running OK, leave this option set at All Steps. If things are bogging down, select one of the lesser percentages from the drop-down list.
   - **Colors using enhanced dither:** Deselect this check box to speed up drawing. Again, this command does not affect printing, just the display on-screen.
   - **Skip startup dialog box:** Check this box to remove that annoying startup "Whatdya wanna do?" dialog box.
   - **Remove excess points from curves pasted from other applications:** That's what it does. Check this box to speed things up and eliminate waste.
   - **Notify linked clients only on save:** If you have embedded files or objects, checking this box reminds the host application to update only if you have changed the object.
   - **Tool lock:** Normally, F/X makes the selection tool active after any action with one of the other tools. Checking this box keeps the current tool active until you select another.

## Preview/Outline

Toggles the view of the active screen between preview and outline modes.

### Digital rodent replacement

### Using Preview/Outline

Choose Preview/Outline from the Window menu to toggle the view of the active screen.

### More stuff

Although you can edit in both views, the outline view does not display fills or the widths of outlines. It is, therefore, lots faster.

## Print Setup

Selects the printer that will be used to print the presentation.

### Using Print setup

1. Choose Print setup from the File menu.
2. Select a printer from the list of installed printers.
3. Choose Setup to open the Windows printer setup dialog box that is specific to the selected printer.

### More stuff

See *Windows 3.1 For Dummies,* 2nd Edition for an explanation of the Control Panel and the Printers dialog box.

## Quick F/X

Creates some really wonderful special effects for you.

### Ribbon bar icon

## Using Quick F/X

1. Select the object to which you want to apply a special effect.
2. Choose Quick F/X from the Effects menu to open the Quick F/X dialog box.

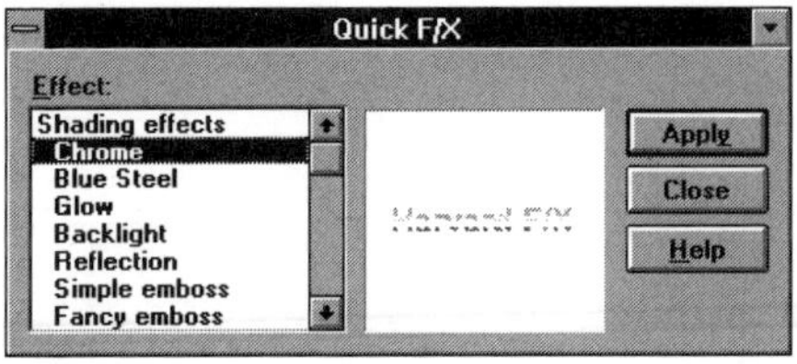


3. Select the effect you want to apply from the drop-down list.

TIP

The special effects come in six different groups: Shading effects, Text effects, Shadows, Fills, Sweeps, and Bitmap effects. You can apply most of these effects to any object, but you obtain the best results by reserving Text and Bitmap effects for those particular formats.

## More stuff

REFERENCE

If you want to apply one of the standard effects to a bitmap, trace it first with the Autotrace tool. See the discussion of this tool in the Part of Tools section of this part.

# Rectangular Copy

This pretty neat command copies a selected object in a pattern of rows and columns.

## Using Rectangular copy

1. Select the object that you want to copy.
2. Choose Rectangular copy from the Effects menu to open the Rectangular Copy dialog box.

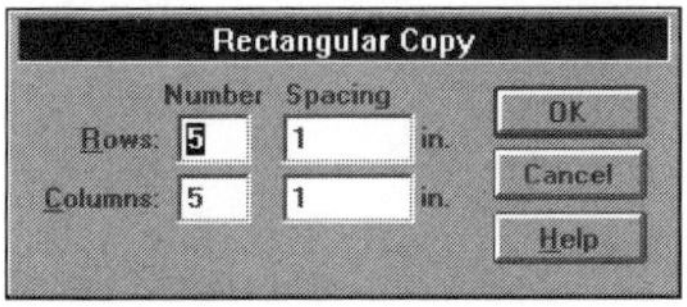

3. Fill in the number of Rows and Columns and the amount of spacing.
4. Click OK.

### More stuff

The spacing measurement is taken from a point on one object to the corresponding point on another. If your object is fat, allow for this in your calculations, or else the rows and columns will overlap.

## Redo

When you change your other mind and want to put something back the way it was before you chose the Undo command, Redo is for you.

### Digital rodent replacement

Ctrl + R

### Using Redo

Choose Redo from the Edit menu. Tough.

### More stuff

The Redo command becomes available only after you issue an Undo command. The wording of the command in the menu changes depending on the last command that was undone.

## Save, Save As

Saves a document to disk. When you save a document for the first time, the Save As dialog box opens to let you give the document a name. Any subsequent save uses the same name, and the Save As dialog box doesn't open. You also can use the Save As command to save an existing file in a different location or under a different name.

### Ribbon bar icon

## Digital rodent replacement

Ctrl + S

## Using Save and Save as

1. Choose Save (or Save as) from the File menu.
2. If you selected Save and the drawing already has a name, the drawing is saved to disk.
3. If this is the first time the drawing has been saved, or if you selected Save as, the Save As dialog box opens.

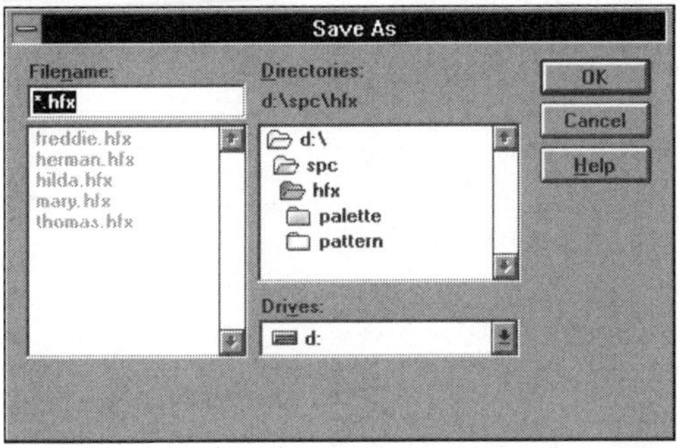


4. Give the file a name and select the drive and directory in which it is to be stored.
5. Click OK.

# Select All

Selects all objects in the drawing, even those that are not shown in the current view.

## Using Select all

Choose Select all from the Edit menu.

# Simplify

Use this command to close paths and create separate path segments wherever two paths cross.

## Using Simplify

1. Select the objects that you want to simplify.
2. Choose Simplify from the Arrange menu.

# Size

Changes the size of text.

## Using Size

1. Choosing Size from the Text menu opens a list of common font sizes. If the one you want is shown, click it to select it.
2. If the size you want is not listed, click Other to open the Select Size dialog box.

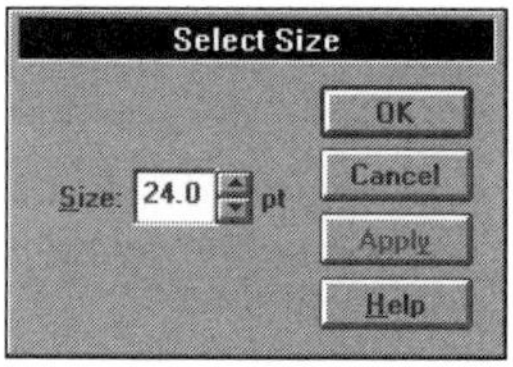


3. Type the Size that you want in the box.
4. Click OK.

## More stuff

See All Attributes (Text) for a way to change more font stuff at once than just the type size.

## Snap F3/F4

### Snap on/off

### To grid and guides

### To points

Toggles Snap to features on and off.

### Digital rodent replacement

Turn on Snap: F3

Turn off Snap: F4

### Using Snap

You toggle the snap master switch on or off by choosing Snap on or Snap off from the Snap flyout menu of the Options menu. (Try saying that ten times fast.)

After Snap has been turned on, you can elect to either "magnetize" (make stuff snap to) the grid and guides, points, or both by clicking the command. You can tell that the command is active when a check mark is next to it in the flyout menu.

## Store

### Store last pt

### Recall last pt

### Store origin

### Recall origin

When you are deeply involved in the creative process, the last thing that you want to worry about is finding your way back home. This command allows you to establish way points (or reference points) to which you can return with a click of the mouse or by pressing a function key.

## Digital rodent replacements

Store last pt: F5

Recall last pt: F6

Store origin: F7

Recall origin: F8

## Using Store

To store your current location, choose Store last pt from the Store flyout menu of the Options menu. To recall that location, choose Recall last pt from the Store flyout menu of the Options menu. To store the current location of the rulers 0,0 points, choose Store origin from the Store flyout menu of the Options menu. To recall that location, choose Recall origin from the Store flyout menu of the Options menu.

## More stuff

The last point is the place where you were when you issued the command.

The origin is the point where both rulers show 0.

# Style

Lets you change the type style.

## Using Style

1. Choose Style from the Text menu to open the Style flyout menu.
2. Select the style that you want.

## More stuff

The styles shown in the flyout menu vary with the font selected. Most common are Regular, Italic, and Bold.

See All Attributes (Text) to find out how to change other font-related stuff, too.

# Text Effects

## Shape to path

## Shape between two paths

## Fit above path

## Fit below path

Warps, stretches, and otherwise dominates text, forcing it to submit to your wishes. The idea is to draw paths by using the drawing tools and to make a text block follow the path's contours.

## Using Text effects

To shape text to a path:

1. Draw the path you want by using one of the drawing tools (freehand, pen, line, arc, rectangle, oval, or polygon).
2. Create the text and assign any attributes that you want to it, such as fill and outline.
3. Select the text and the path by Shift-clicking each.
4. Choose Shape to path from the Text effects flyout menu in the Text menu.

TIP

The text assumes the same relative position as it has to the path before the two were joined. In other words, if the text is above the path, it is shaped to the upper contour; if it is below, it conforms to the bottom of the path.

Left and right measurements work much the same way. Your best bet is to position the text after you create it to the place on the path where you want it to start. Then go ahead and shape it.

To shape text between two paths:

1. Draw the paths that you want by using the drawing tools (freehand, pen, line, arc, rectangle, oval, or polygon).
2. Create the text and assign any attributes that you want to it, such as fill and outline.
3. Select the text and both of the paths by Shift-clicking each.
4. Choose Shape between two paths from the Text effects flyout menu in the Text menu.

See the preceding tip for help in positioning the text on (between) the paths.

To position the text above or below a path:

1. Draw the path you want by using the drawing tools (freehand, pen, line, arc, rectangle, oval, or polygon).
2. Create the text and assign any attributes you want to it, such as fill and outline.
3. Select the text and path by Shift-clicking each.
4. Choose Fit above path or Fit below path from the Text effects flyout menu in the Text menu.

See the preceding tip for help in positioning the text on the paths.

## More stuff

If your text doesn't look just the way you want it to, choose Undo effect from the Edit menu.

# Tile

You can have several images open at the same time. To avoid being sent to bed without your supper because of slovenly screen habits, you may want to have all your pictures neatly tiled, one right next to the other. The Tile command does this automatically, saving you much frustration and many sidelong glances from your peers.

## Digital rodent replacement

Shift + F4

## Using Tile

If you have a deep-seated need to be neat or a disapproving significant other, choose Tile from the Windows menu to display all your open pictures, tidily ordered.

# Undo

Reverses actions that you performed. You can set the number of actions you want F/X to remember (up to 16) in the Preferences dialog box. (Choose Preferences from the Options menu.)

## Digital rodent replacement

Ctrl + Z

## Using Undo

Choose Undo from the Edit menu. The name following the Undo command reflects the next action that can be undone.

# Ungroup

Tears asunder groups that have been put together by using the Group command.

## Ribbon bar icon

## Digital rodent replacement

Ctrl + U

## Using Ungroup

1. Select the group that you want to ungroup.
2. Choose Ungroup from the Arrange menu.

## More stuff

See the Group command to learn how to group stuff so that you can ungroup it later.

# Unlock

Unlocks and selects all that you locked with the Lock command.

## Digital rodent replacement

Ctrl + K

## Using Unlock

Choose Unlock from the Arrange menu.

## More stuff

See the Lock command to learn how to lock stuff so that you can unlock it later.

# Warp

## Add

## Remove

## Permanent

## Copy warp

## Paste warp

Lets you treat a text or path object as if it were a lump of clay, molding it into different shapes by moving the control points about.

## Using Warp

To add warp to an object:

1. Select the object to which you want to apply warp.
2. Choose Add from the Warp flyout menu of the Effects menu. This action selects the select points tool and surrounds the object with handles.
3. Drag the handles in or out to mimic the warp that you want.

To keep your warp uniform throughout your work, see Copy Warp in this section.

To remove warp from an object:

1. Select the object.
2. Choose Remove from the Warp flyout menu of the Effects menu.

To make a warp permanent, so that you can import it into other applications:

1. Select the object.
2. Choose Permanent from the Warp flyout menu of the Effects menu.

To copy warp from one object to another:

1. Select the base object.
2. Choose Copy warp from the Warp flyout menu of the Effects menu.
3. Select the destination object.
4. Choose Paste warp from the Warp flyout menu of the Effects menu.

### More stuff

Choose Quick F/X from the Effects menu to apply a variety of prebuilt special effects.

## The Part of Tools

Harvard F/X has a variety of tools that help you create strange and interesting things. This section of the book discusses each tool in alphabetical order. You will find that the status bar, located in the Title area of the F/X window (strange and interesting, no?), gives you a great deal of assistance with the tools, usually indicating the functions that you can perform with whichever tool you're pointing to.

## Arc Tool

This tool is used to draw lines made up of arcs and straight line segments.

### Using the arc tool

1. Click where you want to start the arc.
2. Click again where you want the radius of the circle to be. This action forms a temporary circle on-screen. You can drag the circle into place by pointing to where you want it to begin and then dragging the mouse.

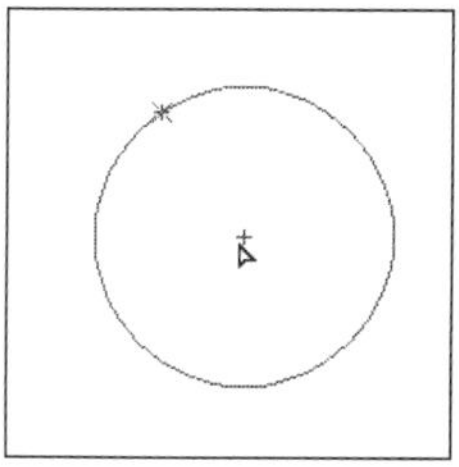

3. Click the temporary circle and drag in or out to select which arc that you want to draw.

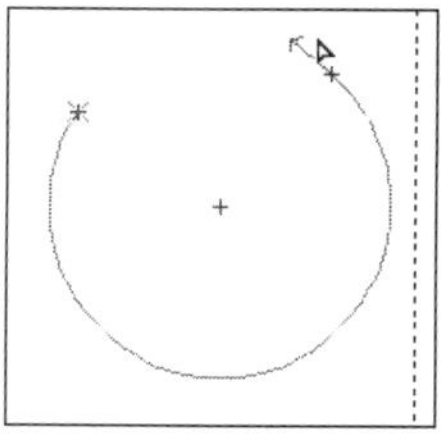

4. Click another tool, or somewhere outside of the arc, to end the path. The temporary circle now assumes the shape of a permanent arc and has the line and fill attributes that were in effect when you started this whole deal.

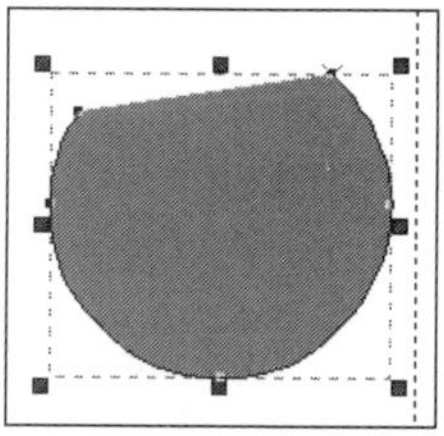

## Rascally rodent's repertoire and magical keyboard moves

Left mouse button: Use this button to drag the endpoint, establishing the size of the arc or line.

Ctrl+left mouse button: Use this combination to draw a straight line.

Shift+left mouse button: Use this combination to constrain the radius of the arc to the Control angle that is set in the Measurements dialog box.

See the Measurements command.

Right mouse button: "I changed my other mind." Back step.

# Autotrace Tool

Use the Autotrace tool to convert bitmaps to raster graphics. This may sound like a mouthful, but after you trace a bitmap, you can rotate, skew, mirror, and use the neato Quick F/X on it.

## Using the Autotrace tool

1. Import the bitmap that you want to trace. (The most common bitmap formats are BMP, TIF, PCX, GIF, and MAC.)

   This is really useful for prettying up a scanned corporate logo, for example.

2. Select the Autotrace tool.
3. Drag a marquee box around the object by holding down the left mouse button while dragging from corner to opposite corner with the Autotrace tool's arrow pointer.

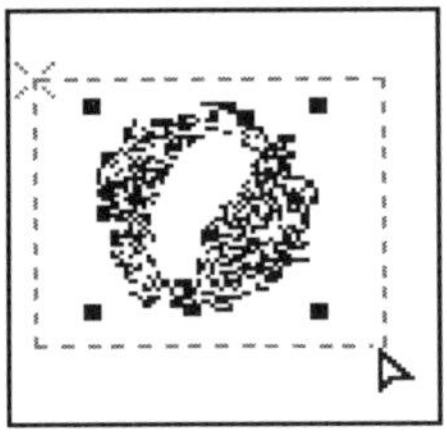

4. Release the mouse button. You now can edit individual line segments, as well as group the whole thing and apply special effects to it.

## Rascally rodent's repertoire and magical keyboard moves

Left mouse button: Press this button to drag a marquee selection box around the bitmap that you want to trace.

Double-click: Double-click the Autotrace tool to open the Autotrace Tool dialog box to adjust various tracing settings.

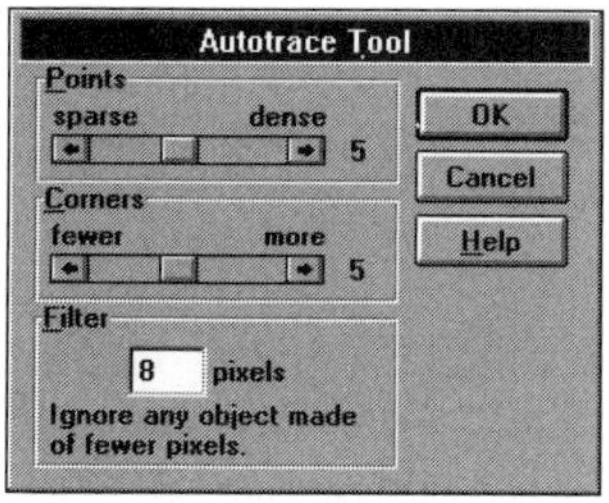


- **Points:** The denser the slider is set, the more closely the tracing follows the bitmap, which can result in a jagged appearance. Set the slider more toward the sparse end to obtain smoother, but less accurate, results.
- **Corners:** High settings place corner points every place that F/X determines the slightest change in direction, which also can result in a jagged look. Set the slider more toward the fewer end to obtain smoother, but less accurate, results.
- **Filter:** Set this number higher (you can go up to 999) to keep F/X from trying to trace every little bug footprint that may be on the image.

# Freehand Tool

Use the freehand tool to draw . . . well, freehand.

## Using the freehand tool

1. Set any line and fill attributes that you may want.
2. Click the freehand tool to select it.
3. Hold down the left mouse button and draw away.

## Rascally rodent's repertoire and magical keyboard moves

Shift+left mouse button: Lets you erase what you just did.

Double-click: Double-click the freehand tool to open the Freehand Tool dialog box.

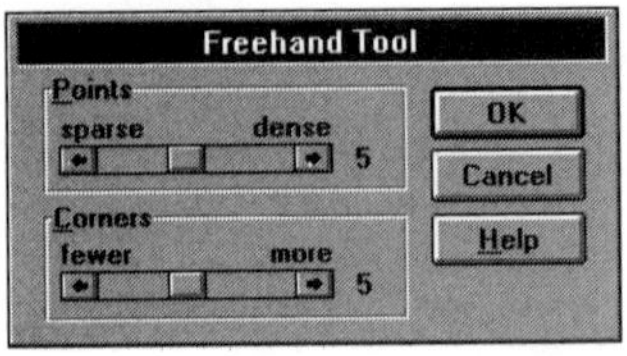


- **Points:** The denser the slider is set, the more closely the line follows your hand movements, which can result in a jagged appearance. Set the slider more toward the sparse end to obtain smoother, but less accurate, results.
- **Corners:** High settings place corner points every place that F/X determines the slightest change in direction, which also can result in a jagged look. Set the slider more toward the fewer end to obtain smoother, but less accurate, results.

# Line Tool

The line tool is used to draw — surprise! — lines. Not just any old lines, though. You can attach bunches of them together to create your masterpiece without even releasing the death grip you have on that poor furry little woodland creature.

## Using the line tool

1. Set whatever line and fill attributes that please you.
2. Click the Line tool to select it.
3. Click the place where you want to start your line.
4. Click where you want the line to end or change direction.
5. Keep clicking until your shape is complete or until you get tired of the exercise.
6. To end the line, select another tool or click the beginning or end of the path.

## Rascally rodent's repertoire and magical keyboard moves

Left mouse button: Use this button to drag a line into place.

Shift+left mouse button: Use this combination to constrain the line to the Control angle that is set in the preset angles Measurements dialog box.

See the Measurements command.

Right mouse button: "I changed my other mind." Opens an eraser so you can undo the line that you just did.

# Mirror Tool

Creates a mirror image of an object.

## Using the mirror tool

1. Select the object that you want to mirror.

   If you are working with text objects, you have to convert them to paths by using the Convert to paths command in the Text menu before you can mirror them.

   If you are working with bitmap images, you need to trace them with the Autotrace tool before you can mirror them.

2. Click the mirror tool. Now, when you move the cursor over any handle on the selected object, the cursor shape changes to a small arrow. This arrow establishes the base point for the mirror and points in the direction that the mirror image will be created.
3. Click the handle that you want to use as the base point.

## Rascally rodent's repertoire and magical keyboard moves

Left mouse button: Executes the mirror.

Ctrl+left mouse button: Executes a mirror around the center of the selected object.

Right mouse button: Executes the mirror, leaving a copy of the object behind.

Ctrl+right mouse button: Executes a mirror around the center of the selected object, leaving a copy of the object behind.

Double-click: Double-clicking the mirror tool opens the Mirror Tool dialog box.

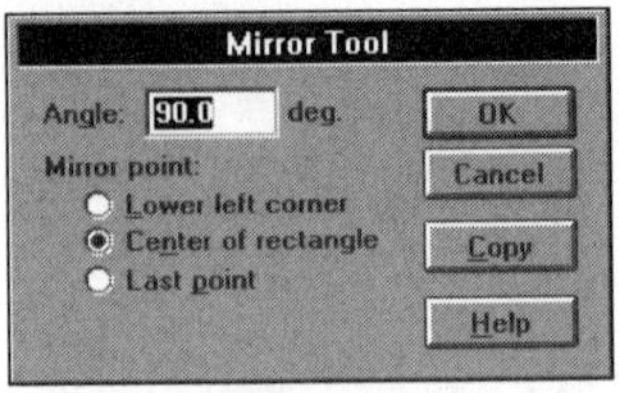


Use this dialog box to set mirroring options. Any changes you make apply the next time you mirror an object.

- **Angle:** Establishes the rotation of a mirrored object. Enter a number from 1 to 359 degrees.
- **Lower left corner:** Sets the mirror point here.
- **Center of rectangle:** Sets the mirror point here.
- **Last point:** Sets the mirror point here.
- **Copy:** Click this button to apply the settings to a copy of the object.

TIP

Double-clicking the object opens the Fill dialog box.

# Oval Tool

Surprise! Use this tool to draw circles and ovals.

## Using the oval tool

1. Set whatever line and fill attributes you want.
2. Select the oval tool.
3. Drag your oval into place. You also can click once where you want it to start and click again where you want it to end. Pretty cool, but it takes a little practice to get everything to come out perfectly.

## Rascally rodent's repertoire and magical keyboard moves

Shift: Press the Shift key while dragging to make a perfect circle.

Ctrl: Press the Ctrl key while dragging to draw your circle or oval from the center out. This way is often lots easier.

## Pen Tool

Use the Pen tool to draw straight lines and smooth curves.

### Using the pen tool

1. Set whatever line and fill attributes you want.
2. Select the pen tool.
3. Click where you want the curve to begin and then keep clicking in kind of a follow-the-dots sort of thing. F/X creates a curve that connects the dots. It's a strange-looking thing called a Bezier curve, but let F/X do all the worrying for you.
4. You can drag a point to show a neat little red arrow that establishes the slope of the Bezier curve. There really is no need to do this, but it looks really geeky and cool.
5. To add a corner point, double-click.

### Rascally rodent's repertoire and magical keyboard moves

Ctrl: Pressing the Ctrl key makes the connections between the last two dots a straight line.

Shift: Pressing the Shift key constrains the radius of the arc to the Control angle that is set in the preset angles Measurements dialog box.

See the Measurements command.

Double-click: Double-clicking establishes a corner point.

Right mouse button: "Oops!" Erases the last segment.

## Polygon Tool

Use this tool to draw objects of many straight sides.

### Using the polygon tool

1. Set whatever line and fill attributes you want.
2. Select the polygon tool.
3. Drag from the center of the polygon to an outside edge. You also can click where you want the center to be and click again where you want it to end.

## Rascally rodent's repertoire and magical keyboard moves

Shift: Press the Shift key while dragging to constrain the sides.

Double-click: Double-click the polygon tool to open the Polygon Tool dialog box.

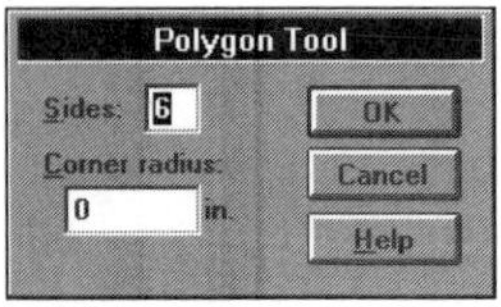


- **Sides:** Type the number of sides that you want your polygon to have.
- **Corner radius:** If you want the corners of the polygon to be rounded, type a measurement here. If you want the corners to be sharp, leave this setting at 0 (zero). For example, typing **.25** produces a polygon with corners rounded to a 1/4-inch radius.

TIP

Double-clicking the object opens the Fill dialog box.

# Rectangle Tool

Use this tool to draw squares and rectangles.

## Using the rectangle tool

1. Set whatever line and fill attributes that you want.
2. Select the rectangle tool.
3. Drag from one corner of the rectangle to the corner diagonally opposite. You also can click where you want the first corner to be and click again where you want it to end.

## Rascally rodent's repertoire and magical keyboard moves

Shift: Press the Shift key while dragging to draw a square.

Ctrl: Press the Ctrl key while you are dragging to draw your square or polygon from the center out.

Double-click: Double-click the rectangle tool to open the Rectangle Tool dialog box.

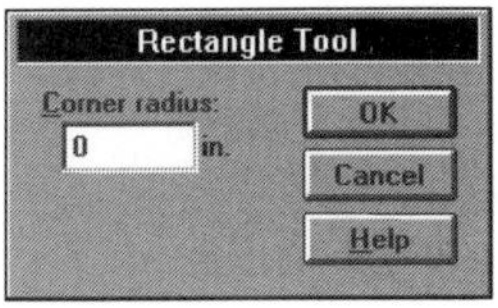


If you want the corners of the square or rectangle to be rounded, type a measurement in the Corner radius box. The next square or rectangle that you draw will have its corners rounded to the radius measurement you selected. If you want the corners to be sharp, leave this setting at 0 (zero).

TIP

Double-clicking the object opens the Fill dialog box.

# Rotate Tool

Use this tool to rotate stuff.

## Using the rotate tool

1. Select the object that you want to rotate.

   TIP

   To rotate text, you must first convert it to paths by using the Convert to Paths command in the Text menu.

   If you are working with bitmap images, you need to trace them with the Autotrace tool before you can rotate them.

2. Click the rotate tool. Now, when you move the cursor over any handle on the selected object, the cursor changes to a small, bent arrow.
3. Drag the object around to rotate it.

## Rascally rodent's repertoire and magical keyboard moves

Shift: Press the Shift key while dragging to constrain the angle to the Control angle that is set in the preset angles Measurements dialog box.

REFERENCE

See the Measurements command.

Right mouse button: Drag with the right mouse button to rotate the object and leave a copy behind.

Double-click: Double-click the rotate tool to open the Rotate Tool dialog box.

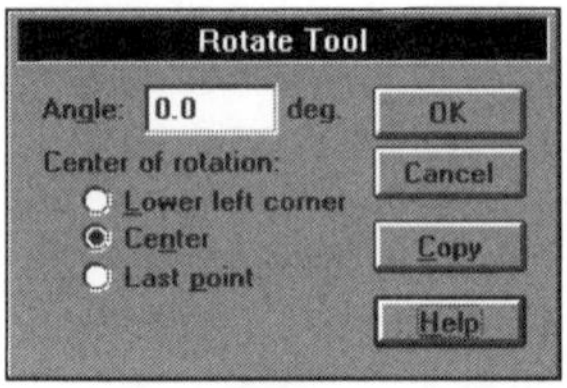


- **Angle:** Enter the angle that you want the object to rotate.
- **Center of rotation:** Choose the place that you want the object to rotate around: Lower left corner, Center, or Last point.
- **Copy:** Click this button to apply the settings and leave a copy behind.

TIP

Double-clicking the object opens the Fill dialog box.

## Select Points Tool

This tool is the sonic screwdriver of Harvard F/X, a tool of many uses that can get you out of lots of trouble. Use the select points tool to edit control points and line segments.

### Using the select points tool

1. Click the select points tool to make it active.

   TIP

   It's a good idea to zoom in on the points that you want to manipulate. It makes them a lot easier to see, and because they are apparently larger, they are easier to select and move.

2. Select the line(s) or control point(s) that you want to edit by either dragging a selection box around them or clicking and Shift-clicking individual points or lines.
3. Selected lines and control points have solid black handles.
4. You can move the selected stuff about. The handles that are black move with you, and the ones that are not black remain anchored in place.
5. You can drag the selected stuff with the mouse or nudge it by using one of the arrow keys on your keyboard.

## Rascally rodent's repertoire and magical keyboard moves

Ctrl+left mouse button: Changes a corner point to a smooth point or vice versa. Or changes a line segment to a curve and back.

Double-click: Double-clicking a line segment opens the Edit Segment dialog box.

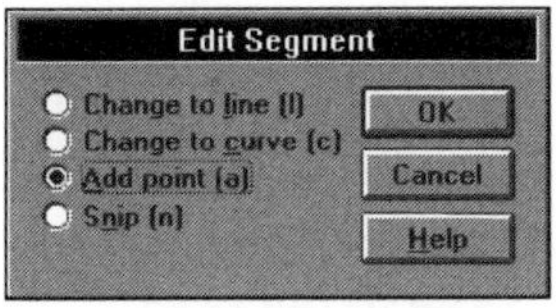


- **Change to line:** Changes the segment to a straight line.
- **Change to curve:** Changes a straight line segment to a curve segment.
- **Add point:** Adds a control point where you click.
- **Snip:** Cuts the segment.

Double-clicking a control point opens the Edit Point dialog box.

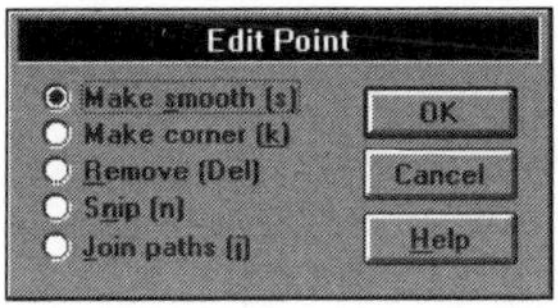


- **Make smooth:** Makes the control point a smooth point. Basically, it removes any radical change in direction from the point. At least one of the two joining segments must be a curve segment for this option to work.
- **Make corner (k):** Creates a corner point.
- **Remove:** Deletes the point.
- **Snip:** Cuts the path at the control point.
- **Join paths:** Joins the two end points. You have to select two path endpoints before using this command.

Double-clicking the object opens the Fill dialog box.

# Selection Tool

You use the selection tool to select an object for moving, resizing, copying, deleting, grouping, and other similar stuff. You have used the tool if selection handles appear around the object.

## Using the selection tool

1. Click the selection tool to make it active.
2. Click an object to select it. To select multiple objects, Shift-click each one, or drag a selection box around them.
3. To scale an object, select it and drag a handle.

   To move an object, select it and drag it to a new location.

   To copy an object, select it and drag with the right mouse button.

## Rascally rodent's repertoire and magical keyboard moves

Left mouse button: Use this button to select objects.

Shift+left mouse button: Use this button to select multiple objects.

Right mouse button: Use it to copy an object.

Double-click: Opens the Scale dialog box.

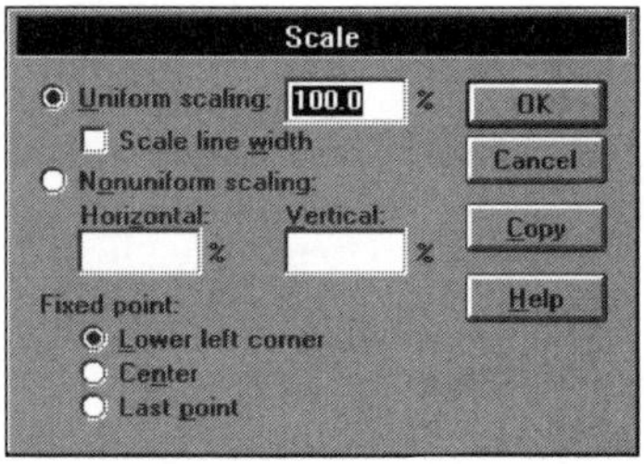


- **Uniform scaling:** Type a percentage from 10 to 1,000 to make all your scaling identical.
- **Scale line width:** Click this check box if you want the line to scale fatter and thinner with the object.
- **Nonuniform scaling:** Type percentages for the Horizontal and Vertical scaling if you want the two parameters to be different.

- **Fixed point:** Select the point from which you want the object to shrink or grow: Lower left corner, Center, or Last point.
- **Copy:** Click this button to leave a copy of the original object behind.

TIP

Double-clicking the object opens the Fill dialog box.

## Skew Tool

Use this tool to slant or keystone your object. (*Keystone* means to stretch or shrink one side of the object, creating a perspective effect.)

### Using the skew tool

1. Select the object that you want to skew.

   TIP

   It's a good idea to zoom in on the object that you want to manipulate. It makes it a lot easier to see and mess with.

   TIP

   If you want to skew or keystone bitmaps, you need to Autotrace them first. If you want to skew or keystone text objects, you need to convert them to paths.

2. Click the skew tool. The object is now surrounded by handles.
3. Keystone the object by dragging one of the four corner handles in or out. Skew the object by dragging one of the four side handles.

### Rascally rodent's repertoire and magical keyboard moves

Shift: Press the Shift key to constrain a skew or keystone to the Control angle that is set in the preset angles Measurements dialog box.

REFERENCE

See the Measurements command.

Right mouse button: Drag the skew or keystone with the right mouse button to create a copy of the original object.

Double-click: Double-click the skew tool to open the Skew Tool dialog box.

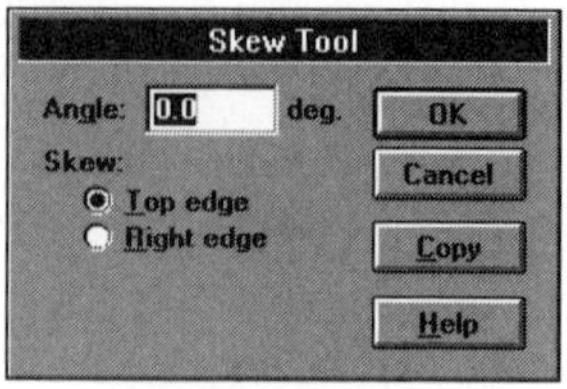


- **Angle:** Enter the desired angle, from 1 to 359 degrees, measured counterclockwise.
- **Skew:** Select the points that you want to use, Top edge or Right edge.
- **Copy:** Click the copy button to create a copy of the original object.

TIP

Double-clicking the object opens the Fill dialog box.

# Text Tool

Use the text tool to insert or edit text.

## Using the text tool

To create text:

1. Select the text tool.
2. Click the I-beam cursor where you want the text to appear. This action forms a text box.
3. Type away. When you have finished entering your text, select another tool or create another text entry.

To edit text:

1. Select the text tool.
2. Click the cursor in the text box.
3. Select the text that you want to edit by dragging over it.

   TIP

   To select a single word, double-click it.
4. Delete the text by using the Del key, or replace it by typing over it.
5. To change the attributes of the text, choose All attributes from the Text menu.

### Rascally rodent's repertoire and magical keyboard moves

Double-click: Double-click the text tool to open the Text Attributes dialog box. This dialog box can be used to change the defaults (which attributes will be applied the next time you insert text). To change the attributes of any selected text, choose All attributes from the Text menu.

See All Attributes in the F/X command reference.

## Zoom Tool

Get up close and personal with what you are looking at, or step back and get an overview.

### Using the zoom tool

1. Click the zoom tool.
2. Click the left mouse button to zoom in, and the right mouse button to zoom out.

### Rascally rodent's repertoire and magical keyboard moves

Left mouse button: Zoom in.

You can reposition your view by dragging the screen. When you press and hold down the left mouse button, the cursor changes into a hand. When you drag the hand around, a funny-looking line is drawn on-screen; releasing the mouse button repositions the view to the area. It's difficult to explain. Try it.

Right mouse button: Zoom out.

Shift: You can set two zoom levels in the Zoom Tool dialog box. Holding down the Shift key and clicking the left or right mouse button changes your view between the two selections.

Shift+left mouse button: Hold down the Shift key and drag a box around the area that you want to zoom in on.

Double-click: Double-click the zoom tool to open the Zoom Tool dialog box.

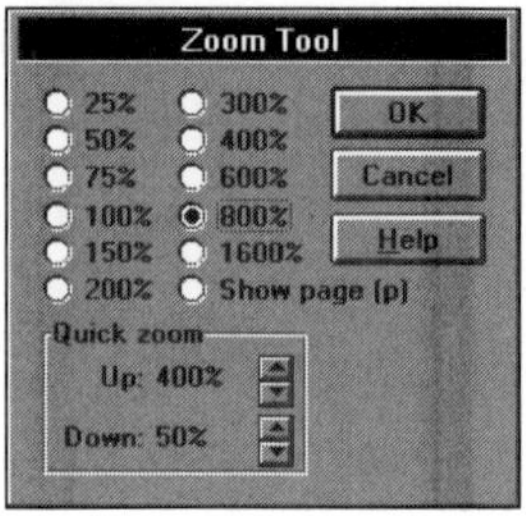


Select the level of zoom you want by clicking one of the radio buttons.

Change the level of Quick Zoom (see Shift in the "Rascally rodent's repertoire and magical keyboard moves" section) by selecting new numbers to assign to the Shift+left mouse button (Up) and the Shift+right mouse button (Down) in the spinner boxes.

# Index

## • C •

## • D •



## • E •

## • F •

## • G •

## • H •



## • I •

## • J •



## • L •



## • M •

## • N •



## • O •

## • P •

## • Q •



## • R •

## • S •

## • T •

## • U •

## • V •



## • W •



## • X •



## • Y •



## • Z •

# Notes

## Notes

| Title | Author | ISBN | Price |
|---|---|---|---|
| **DATABASE (continued)** | | | |
| dBASE For Windows For Dummies™ | by Scott Palmer | 1-56884-179-5 | $19.95 USA/$26.95 Canada |
| dBASE 5 For Windows Programming For Dummies™ | by Ted Coombs & Jason Coombs | 1-56884-215-5 | $19.99 USA/$26.99 Canada |
| FoxPro 2.6 For Windows For Dummies™ | by John Kaufeld | 1-56884-187-6 | $19.95 USA/$26.95 Canada |
| Paradox 5 For Windows For Dummies™ | by John Kaufeld | 1-56884-185-X | $19.95 USA/$26.95 Canada |
| **DESKTOP PUBLISHING / ILLUSTRATION / GRAPHICS** | | | |
| CorelDRAW! 5 For Dummies™ | by Deke McClelland | 1-56884-157-4 | $19.95 USA/$26.95 Canada |
| CorelDRAW! For Dummies™ | by Deke McClelland | 1-56884-042-X | $19.95 USA/$26.95 Canada |
| Harvard Graphics 2 For Windows For Dummies™ | by Roger C. Parker | 1-56884-092-6 | $19.95 USA/$26.95 Canada |
| PageMaker 5 For Macs For Dummies™ | by Galen Gruman | 1-56884-178-7 | $19.95 USA/$26.95 Canada |
| PageMaker 5 For Windows For Dummies™ | by Deke McClelland & Galen Gruman | 1-56884-160-4 | $19.95 USA/$26.95 Canada |
| QuarkXPress 3.3 For Dummies™ | by Galen Gruman & Barbara Assadi | 1-56884-217-1 | $19.99 USA/$26.99 Canada |
| **FINANCE / PERSONAL FINANCE / TEST TAKING REFERENCE** | | | |
| QuickBooks 3 For Dummies™ | by Stephen L. Nelson | 1-56884-227-9 | $19.99 USA/$26.99 Canada |
| Quicken 8 For DOS For Dummies™, 2nd Edition | by Stephen L. Nelson | 1-56884-210-4 | $19.95 USA/$26.95 Canada |
| Quicken 5 For Macs For Dummies™ | by Stephen L. Nelson | 1-56884-211-2 | $19.95 USA/$26.95 Canada |
| Quicken 4 For Windows For Dummies™, 2nd Edition | by Stephen L. Nelson | 1-56884-209-0 | $19.95 USA/$26.95 Canada |
| The SAT I For Dummies™ | by Suzee Vlk | 1-56884-213-9 | $14.95 USA/$20.99 Canada |
| **GROUPWARE / INTEGRATED** | | | |
| Lotus Notes 3/3.1 For Dummies™ | by Paul Freeland & Stephen Londergan | 1-56884-212-0$ | $19.95 USA/$26.95 Canada |
| Microsoft Office 4 For Windows For Dummies™ | by Roger C. Parker | 1-56884-183-3 | $19.95 USA/$26.95 Canada |
| Microsoft Works 3 For Windows For Dummies™ | by David C. Kay | 1-56884-214-7 | $19.99 USA/$26.99 Canada |
| **INTERNET / COMMUNICATIONS / NETWORKING** | | | |
| CompuServe Starter Kits For Dummies™ | by Wallace Wang | 1-56884-181-7 | $19.95 USA/$26.95 Canada |
| Modems For Dummies™, 2nd Edition | by Tina Rathbone | 1-56884-223-6 | $19.99 USA/$26.99 Canada |
| Modems For Dummies™ | by Tina Rathbone | 1-56884-001-2 | $19.95 USA/$26.95 Canada |
| MORE Internet For Dummies™ | by John R. Levine & Margaret L.Young | 1-56884-164-7 | $19.95 USA/$26.95 Canada |
| NetWare For Dummies™ | by Ed Tittel & Deni Connor | 1-56884-003-9 | $19.95 USA/$26.95 Canada |
| Networking For Dummies™ | by Doug Lowe | 1-56884-079-9 | $19.95 USA/$26.95 Canada |
| ProComm Plus 2 For Windows For Dummies™ | by Wallace Wang | 1-56884-219-8 | $19.99 USA/$26.99 Canada |

11/11/94

# DUMMIES PRESS

## The fun & easy way to learn about computers and more!

**Windows 3.1 For Dummies,™ 2nd Edition**
*by Andy Rathbone*

1-56884-182-5
$16.95 USA/$22.95 Canada

**The Internet For Dummies,™ 2nd Edition**
*by John R. Levine & Carol Baroudi*

1-56884-222-8
$19.95 USA/$26.99 Canada

**DOS For Dummies,® 2nd Edition**
*by Dan Gookin*

1-878058-75-4
$16.95 USA/$21.95 Canada

**Personal Finance For Dummies™**
*by Eric Tyson*

1-56884-150-7
$16.95 USA/$21.95 Canada

**PCs For Dummies,™ 2nd Edition**
*by Dan Gookin & Andy Rathbone*

1-56884-078-0
$16.95 USA/$21.95 Canada

**MORE Windows For Dummies,™**
*by Andy Rathbone*

1-56884-048-9
$19.95 USA/$26.95 Canada

**Macs For Dummies,® 2nd Edition**
*by David Pogue*

1-56884-051-9
$19.95 USA/$26.95 Canada

**WordPerfect For Windows For Dummies™**
*by Margaret Levine & David C. Kay*

1-56884-032-2
$16.95 USA/$21.95 Canada

### Here's a complete listing of IDG's *...For Dummies* Titles

| Title | Author | ISBN | Price |
|---|---|---|---|
| **DATABASE** | | | |
| Access 2 For Dummies™ | by Scott Palmer | 1-56884-090-X | $19.95 USA/$26.95 Canada |
| Access Programming For Dummies™ | by Rob Krumm | 1-56884-091-8 | $19.95 USA/$26.95 Canada |
| Approach 3 For Windows For Dummies™ | by Doug Lowe | 1-56884-233-3 | $19.99 USA/$26.99 Canada |
| dBASE For DOS For Dummies™ | by Scott Palmer & Michael Stabler | 1-56884-188-4 | $19.95 USA/$26.95 Canada |

11/11/94

**FOR MORE INFO OR TO ORDER, PLEASE CALL ▸ 800. 762. 2974**

For volume discounts & special orders please call Tony Real, Special Sales, at 415. 312. 0650

| Title | Author | ISBN | Price |
|---|---|---|---|
| **INTERNET / COMMUNICATIONS / NETWORKING (continued)** | | | |
| The Internet For Dummies™, 2nd Edition | by John R. Levine & Carol Baroudi | 1-56884-222-8 | $19.99 USA/$26.99 Canada |
| The Internet For Macs For Dummies™ | by Charles Seiter | 1-56884-184-1 | $19.95 USA/$26.95 Canada |
| **MACINTOSH** | | | |
| Macs For Dummies®, 2nd Edition | by David Pogue | 1-56884-173-6 | $19.95 USA/$26.95 Canada |
| Macs Programming For Dummies™ | by Dan Parks Sydow | 1-56884-173-6 | $19.95 USA/$26.95 Canada |
| Macintosh System 7.5 For Dummies™ | by Bob LeVitus | 1-56884-197-3 | $19.95 USA/$26.95 Canada |
| MORE Macs For Dummies® | by David Pogue | 1-56884-087-X | $19.95 USA/$26.95 Canada |
| PageMaker 5 For Macs For Dummies™ | by Galen Gruman | 1-56884-178-7 | $19.95 USA/$26.95 Canada |
| QuarkXPress 3.3 For Dummies™ | by Galen Gruman & Barbara Assadi | 1-56884-217-1 | $19.99 USA/$26.99 Canada |
| Upgrading and Fixing Macs For Dummies™ | by Kearney Rietmann & Frank Higgins | 1-56884-189-2 | $19.95 USA/$26.95 Canada |
| **MULTIMEDIA** | | | |
| Multimedia & CD-ROMs For Dummies™ Interactive Multimedia Value Pack | by Andy Rathbone | 1-56884-225-2 | $29.95 USA/$39.95 Canada |
| Multimedia & CD-ROMs For Dummies™ | by Andy Rathbone | 1-56884-089-6 | $19.95 USA/$26.95 Canada |
| **OPERATING SYSTEMS / DOS** | | | |
| MORE DOS For Dummies® | by Dan Gookin | 1-56884-046-2 | $19.95 USA/$26.95 Canada |
| S.O.S. For DOS™ | by Katherine Murray | 1-56884-043-8 | $12.95 USA/$16.95 Canada |
| OS/2 For Dummies™ | by Andy Rathbone | 1-878058-76-2 | $19.95 USA/$26.95 Canada |
| **UNIX** | | | |
| UNIX For Dummies™ | by John R. Levine & Margaret Levine Young | 1-878058-58-4 | $19.95 USA/$26.95 Canada |
| **WINDOWS** | | | |
| S.O.S. For Windows™ | by Katherine Murray | 1-56884-045-4 | $12.95 USA/$16.95 Canada |
| MORE Windows "X" For Dummies™, 3rd Edition | by Andy Rathbone | 1-56884-240-6 | $19.99 USA/$26.99 Canada |
| **PCs / HARDWARE** | | | |
| Illustrated Computer Dictionary For Dummies™ | by Dan Gookin, Wally Wang, & Chris Van Buren | 1-56884-004-7 | $12.95 USA/$16.95 Canada |
| Upgrading and Fixing PCs For Dummies™ | by Andy Rathbone | 1-56884-002-0 | $19.95 USA/$26.95 Canada |
| AutoCAD For Dummies™ | by Bud Smith | 1-56884-191-4 | $19.95 USA/$26.95 Canada |
| PowerPoint 4 For Windows For Dummies™ | by Doug Lowe | 1-56884-161-2 | $16.95 USA/$22.95 Canada |
| **PRESENTATION / AUTOCAD / PROGRAMMING** | | | |
| Borland C++ For Dummies™ | by Michael Hyman | 1-56884-162-0 | $19.95 USA/$26.95 Canada |
| "Borland's New Language Product" For Dummies™ | by Neil Rubenking | 1-56884-200-7 | $19.95 USA/$26.95 Canada |

11/11/94

| Title | Author | ISBN | Price |
|---|---|---|---|
| **PRESENTATION / AUTOCAD / PROGRAMMING (continued)** | | | |
| C For Dummies™ | by Dan Gookin | 1-878058-78-9 | $19.95 USA/$26.95 Canada |
| C++ For Dummies™ | by Stephen R. Davis | 1-56884-163-9 | $19.95 USA/$26.95 Canada |
| Mac Programming For Dummies™ | by Dan Parks Sydow | 1-56884-173-6 | $19.95 USA/$26.95 Canada |
| QBasic Programming For Dummies™ | by Douglas Hergert | 1-56884-093-4 | $19.95 USA/$26.95 Canada |
| Visual Basic "X" For Dummies™, 2nd Edition | by Wallace Wang | 1-56884-230-9 | $19.99 USA/$26.99 Canada |
| Visual Basic 3 For Dummies™ | by Wallace Wang | 1-56884-076-4 | $19.95 USA/$26.95 Canada |
| **SPREADSHEET** | | | |
| 1-2-3 For Dummies™ | by Greg Harvey | 1-878058-60-6 | $16.95 USA/$21.95 Canada |
| 1-2-3 For Windows 5 For Dummies™, 2nd Edition | by John Walkenbach | 1-56884-216-3 | $16.95 USA/$21.95 Canada |
| 1-2-3 For Windows For Dummies™ | by John Walkenbach | 1-56884-052-7 | $16.95 USA/$21.95 Canada |
| Excel 5 For Macs For Dummies™ | by Greg Harvey | 1-56884-186-8 | $19.95 USA/$26.95 Canada |
| Excel For Dummies™, 2nd Edition | by Greg Harvey | 1-56884-050-0 | $16.95 USA/$21.95 Canada |
| MORE Excel 5 For Windows For Dummies™ | by Greg Harvey | 1-56884-207-4 | $19.95 USA/$26.95 Canada |
| Quattro Pro 6 For Windows For Dummies™ | by John Walkenbach | 1-56884-174-4 | $19.95 USA/$26.95 Canada |
| Quattro Pro For DOS For Dummies™ | by John Walkenbach | 1-56884-023-3 | $16.95 USA/$21.95 Canada |
| **UTILITIES** | | | |
| Norton Utilities 8 For Dummies™ | by Beth Slick | 1-56884-166-3 | $19.95 USA/$26.95 Canada |
| **VCRs / CAMCORDERS** | | | |
| VCRs & Camcorders For Dummies™ | by Andy Rathbone & Gordon McComb | 1-56884-229-5 | $14.99 USA/$20.99 Canada |
| **WORD PROCESSING** | | | |
| Ami Pro For Dummies™ | by Jim Meade | 1-56884-049-7 | $19.95 USA/$26.95 Canada |
| MORE Word For Windows 6 For Dummies™ | by Doug Lowe | 1-56884-165-5 | $19.95 USA/$26.95 Canada |
| MORE WordPerfect 6 For Windows For Dummies™ | by Margaret Levine Young & David C. Kay | 1-56884-206-6 | $19.95 USA/$26.95 Canada |
| MORE WordPerfect 6 For DOS For Dummies™ | by Wallace Wang, edited by Dan Gookin | 1-56884-047-0 | $19.95 USA/$26.95 Canada |
| S.O.S. For WordPerfect™ | by Katherine Murray | 1-56884-053-5 | $12.95 USA/$16.95 Canada |
| Word 6 For Macs For Dummies™ | by Dan Gookin | 1-56884-190-6 | $19.95 USA/$26.95 Canada |
| Word For Windows 6 For Dummies™ | by Dan Gookin | 1-56884-075-6 | $16.95 USA/$21.95 Canada |
| Word For Windows For Dummies™ | by Dan Gookin | 1-878058-86-X | $16.95 USA/$21.95 Canada |
| WordPerfect 6 For Dummies™ | by Dan Gookin | 1-878058-77-0 | $16.95 USA/$21.95 Canada |
| WordPerfect For Dummies™ | by Dan Gookin | 1-878058-52-5 | $16.95 USA/$21.95 Canada |
| WordPerfect For Windows For Dummies™ | by Margaret Levine Young & David C. Kay | 1-56884-032-2 | $16.95 USA/$21.95 Canada |

11/11/94

# ORDER FORM

Order Center: **(800) 762-2974** (8 a.m.–6 p.m., EST, weekdays)

*For large quantities call for shipping & handling charges. **Prices are subject to change without notice.

| Qty | ISBN | Title | Price | Total |
|---|---|---|---|---|
| | | | | |
| | | | | |
| | | | | |
| | | | | |
| | | | | |
| | | | | |
| | | | | |
| | | | | |
| | | | | |
| | | | | |
| | | | | |
| | | | | |

*Shipping & Handling Charges*

| | Description | First book | Each additional book | Total |
|---|---|---|---|---|
| *Domestic* | Normal | $4.50 | $1.50 | $ |
| | Two Day Air | $8.50 | $2.50 | $ |
| | Overnight | $18.00 | $3.00 | $ |
| *International* | Surface | $8.00 | $8.00 | $ |
| | Airmail | $16.00 | $16.00 | $ |
| | DHL Air | $17.00 | $17.00 | $ |

IDG BOOKS

Please send this order form to:
IDG Books
7260 Shadeland Station
Suite 100
Indianapolis, IN 46256

Allow up to 3 weeks for delivery. Thank you!

**Ship to:**

Name ____________________

Company ____________________

Address ____________________

City/State/Zip ____________________

Daytime Phone ____________________

**Payment:**

☐ Check to IDG Books (US Funds Only)

☐ VISA

☐ MasterCard

☐ American Express

Card # ____________________

Exp. ____________________

Sign. ____________________

**Subtotal** ________

CA residents add applicable sales tax ________

IN, MA, and MD residents add 5% sales tax ________

IL residents add 6.25% sales tax ________

RI residents add 7% sales tax ________

TX residents add 8.25% sales tax ________

Shipping ________

**Total** ________

11/11/94

# IDG BOOKS WORLDWIDE REGISTRATION CARD

RETURN THIS REGISTRATION CARD FOR FREE CATALOG

**Title of this book:** Harvard Graphics For Windows For Dummies QR

**My overall rating of this book:** ❑ Very good [1] ❑ Good [2] ❑ Satisfactory [3] ❑ Fair [4] ❑ Poor [5]

**How I first heard about this book:**

❑ Found in bookstore; name: [6] ❑ Book review: [7]

❑ Advertisement: [8] ❑ Catalog: [9]

❑ Word of mouth; heard about book from friend, co-worker, etc.: [10] ❑ Other: [11]

**What I liked most about this book:**

**What I would change, add, delete, etc., in future editions of this book:**

**Other comments:**

**Number of computer books I purchase in a year:** ❑ 1 [12] ❑ 2-5 [13] ❑ 6-10 [14] ❑ More than 10 [15]

**I would characterize my computer skills as:** ❑ Beginner [16] ❑ Intermediate [17] ❑ Advanced [18] ❑ Professional [19]

**I use** ❑ DOS [20] ❑ Windows [21] ❑ OS/2 [22] ❑ Unix [23] ❑ Macintosh [24] ❑ Other: [25] ____________ (please specify)

**I would be interested in new books on the following subjects:**
(please check all that apply, and use the spaces provided to identify specific software)

❑ Word processing: [26] ❑ Spreadsheets: [27]

❑ Data bases: [28] ❑ Desktop publishing: [29]

❑ File Utilities: [30] ❑ Money management: [31]

❑ Networking: [32] ❑ Programming languages: [33]

❑ Other: [34]

**I use a PC at** (please check all that apply): ❑ home [35] ❑ work [36] ❑ school [37] ❑ other: [38] ____________

**The disks I prefer to use are** ❑ 5.25 [39] ❑ 3.5 [40] ❑ other: [41] ____________

**I have a CD ROM:** ❑ yes [42] ❑ no [43]

**I plan to buy or upgrade computer hardware this year:** ❑ yes [44] ❑ no [45]

**I plan to buy or upgrade computer software this year:** ❑ yes [46] ❑ no [47]

Name: Business title: [48]

Type of Business: [49]

Address (❑ home [50] ❑ work [51]/Company name: )

Street/Suite#

City [52]/State [53]/Zipcode [54]: Country [55]

❑ **I liked this book!**
You may quote me by name in future IDG Books Worldwide promotional materials.

My daytime phone number is ____________

IDG BOOKS®

THE WORLD OF COMPUTER KNOWLEDGE

❑ **YES!**

**Please keep me informed about IDG's World of Computer Knowledge. Send me the latest IDG Books catalog.**



NO POSTAGE NECESSARY IF MAILED IN THE UNITED STATES

**BUSINESS REPLY MAIL**

FIRST CLASS MAIL PERMIT NO. 2605 SAN MATEO, CALIFORNIA

***IDG Books Worldwide***
***155 Bovet Rd***
***San Mateo CA 94402-9833***